Enlightened Aboriginal Futures

This book examines the radical intervention of the German-Australian Lutheran missionary F. W. Albrecht in the education of Aboriginal children. Albrecht's ideas about consent, freedom of choice and personal autonomy were expressed in schemes designed to educate and empower Aboriginal people and efforts to find Aboriginal futures through education, training and employment.

This book explores how Aboriginal people understood Albrecht's work and the Enlightenment concepts on which it was based. In the context of an Anglo-Australian settler-colonialism that sought to systematically remove the freedom and autonomy of Indigenous people, this study demonstrates how those who participated in the Albrecht scheme were able to reconstruct themselves in ways that fused their own Aboriginal culture and identity with the ideas and values imported from an enlightened Germany.

This book will appeal to students and scholars of cultural history, colonialism, Lutheranism, race and ethnicity and Indigenous studies. It will also be illuminating reading to policymakers searching for a deeper understanding of colonial interventions in Indigenous communities.

Barry Judd, Professor and Director, Indigenous Studies, and Deputy Vice Chancellor Indigenous, The University of Melbourne, Australia.

Katherine Ellinghaus, Associate Professor of History, Department of Archaeology and History, La Trobe University, Australia.

Short Takes on Long Views

Series Editors: *Peter Otto, Clara Tuite, and Elias Greig*

Contemporary notions of reason, imagination, literature, science, sexuality, democracy, Nature and even the Human were forged by Enlightenment and Romantic thought. Yet this inheritance now seems unseated by developments it has helped engineer: the digital revolution, globalisation, climate change, fake news, and the emergence of artificial intelligence.

In this time of rapid change, *Short Takes on Long Views* aims to re-address and re-envision the founding of modernity, its contemporary legacies, and the multiple futures. The series puts the so-called "universal" ideas of the European Enlightenment (and subsequent Romantic responses and revisions) into a global context to transform their histories and legacies in the present, and to imagine new possibilities for the future.

Short Takes on Long Views presents small books on big questions, which will to appeal to both researchers and students across the Humanities and Social Sciences.

Enlightened Aboriginal Futures
Barry Judd and Katherine Ellinghaus

Enlightened Aboriginal Futures

Barry Judd and
Katherine Ellinghaus

LONDON AND NEW YORK

First published 2024
by Routledge
4 Park Square, Milton Park, Abingdon, Oxon OX14 4RN

and by Routledge
605 Third Avenue, New York, NY 10158

Routledge is an imprint of the Taylor & Francis Group, an informa business

@ 2024 Barry Judd and Katherine Ellinghaus

The right of Barry Judd and Katherine Ellinghaus to be identified as authors of this work has been asserted in accordance with sections 77 and 78 of the Copyright, Designs and Patents Act 1988.

All rights reserved. No part of this book may be reprinted or reproduced or utilised in any form or by any electronic, mechanical, or other means, now known or hereafter invented, including photocopying and recording, or in any information storage or retrieval system, without permission in writing from the publishers.

Trademark notice: Product or corporate names may be trademarks or registered trademarks, and are used only for identification and explanation without intent to infringe.

British Library Cataloguing-in-Publication Data
A catalogue record for this book is available from the British Library

ISBN: 9781032251172 (hbk)
ISBN: 9781032251189 (pbk)
ISBN: 9781003281634 (ebk)

DOI: 10.4324/9781003281634

Typeset in Galliard
by codeMantra

This book is dedicated to Lorna Wilson and all the other children who went through the education scheme it describes, whose lives were enriched by their interactions with F. W. Albrecht and who continue to love, respect and admire him.

Contents

List of Figures	*xi*
Acknowledgements	*xiii*

Introduction   1
BARRY JUDD AND KATHERINE ELLINGHAUS

1   **Made in Germany: The Import of Lutheranism and
Enlightenment in Central Australia**   16
BARRY JUDD

*Religious Asylum Seekers: The Coming of Old Lutheran
     Mission to Colonial South Australia 20
Lutheran Reformation: A Precursor to
     German Enlightenment 27*

2   **Albrecht, Hermannsburg and the 'Problem of Work'**   48
BARRY JUDD

*Albrecht: Securing an Aboriginal Future 51
Pathways to Economic Freedom and
     Cultural Autonomy 55*

3   **Mparntwe and the Mission Block: Albrecht's
Education Scheme for Aboriginal Girls**   67
KATHERINE ELLINGHAUS

*The Mission Block 68
Albrecht's Education Scheme 72
A Co-Designed Scheme 75*

viii *Contents*

4 Enlightened Girls: The Scheme in Action   84
KATHERINE ELLINGHAUS

Albrecht's Scheme and Government Policy 85
Enlightened Relationships 92

Conclusion   104
KATHERINE ELLINGHAUS AND BARRY JUDD

Index   *111*

Warning

Aboriginal and Torres Strait Islander readers are warned that this book contains images of Aboriginal people who are now deceased.

Figures

I.1	Pastor and Mrs F.W. Albrecht and family. Courtesy of the Lutheran Archives	6
I.2	'In the schoolroom at Hermannsburg.' Courtesy of the Lutheran Archives	9
1.1	'Maryvale, NT, Finke River Mission Rev FW Albrecht, right, distributing rations of dried fruit, peas etc. to local people for cash sales at reasonable prices.' Courtesy of the Lutheran Archives	20
2.1	'Making boots.' Courtesy of the Lutheran Archives	59
2.2	'Tanning Time.' Courtesy of the Lutheran Archives	60
3.1	'Finke River Mission, NT, Alice Springs. The old church with its bell at the front. 1950s.' Courtesy of the Lutheran Archives	70
3.2	'Alice Springs Lutheran Store, Mbanta'. (Mparntwe). Courtesy of the Lutheran Archives	71
4.1	'The Mission Truck beside the Lutheran Church, Gap Road, Alice Springs, NT'. Courtesy of the Lutheran Archives	93
4.2	An excerpt from 'Success Story,' an article in *The Lutheran* in 1968 detailing the achievements of two of the scheme participants. Courtesy of the Lutheran Archives	96
5.1	Lorna Wilson and Katherine Ellinghaus in the Old Lutheran Church, Mparntwe (Alice Springs), May 2021. Photograph reproduced courtesy of Katherine Ellinghaus	108

Acknowledgements

The authors would like to thank Peter Otto for his suggestions and invitation to contribute this story into a space for which it would not normally be considered. We also thank Olga Radke, for her support of this project and for her ongoing work preserving the history of the Finke River Mission, Beth Marsden for her expert research assistance and Bethany Phillips-Peddlesden for her accomplished assistance in editing the manuscript. The creation of this book was supported by ARC DP200103269.

Introduction

Barry Judd and Katherine Ellinghaus

The Enlightenment is normally a topic that concerns scholars in Philosophy Departments or those who engage with the history of ideas in Politics, Art and Literature. The focus is almost always exclusively European in scope. There is often little or no connection to the history of Australia or contemporary Australian society and how we understand issues as diverse as national identity and global climate change.[1] Given this academic landscape, this book, written from the perspective of scholars writing in the disciplines of Indigenous History and Indigenous Studies, may seem like an unlikely addition to the study of the Enlightenment. Yet both our disciplines engage with the Enlightenment as a necessity: the history in Australia of race relations between Indigenous peoples and British imperialism and settler colonialism begins in the last quarter of the eighteenth century and coincides with the high point of what we refer to today as the European Enlightenment. Indeed, the history of contemporary Australia is so deeply entangled with the emergence of Enlightenment ideas that one cannot be understood without the other.

British colonialism in Australia was primarily motivated by the loss of the thirteen colonies in North America at the conclusion of the American War of Independence. The American colonists were inspired to revolution by radical ideas of liberty adopted directly from the mainstream currents of Enlightenment thinking.[2] The loss of its colonial possessions in North America required the British Empire to find new places for the transportation of England's criminal class, with New South Wales (as the British came to know the eastern half of the southern continent) being selected. Considered in this way, we might then argue that the emergence of contemporary Australia and the interactions between Indigenous peoples and those of settler origins are the outcomes of political actions motivated by the age of Enlightenment and the writings of its key thinkers – Jean-Jacques Rousseau, Voltaire (born François-Marie Arouet), Thomas Paine, Immanuel Kant, David Hume, Georg Wilhelm Friedrich Hegel and many others. The links between the

DOI: 10.4324/9781003281634-1

2 *Barry Judd and Katherine Ellinghaus*

origins of contemporary Australia and the Enlightenment become even more apparent when we investigate the character of leading British imperialist/colonists and their understanding of politics, society and culture and the relationship between the peoples of Europe and those elsewhere. For example, the journal entries of Lieutenant James Cook RN, the so-called 'discoverer' of New South Wales, reflected those Enlightenment philosophies that understand the differences between the peoples of the world primarily through the lens of culture and nurture and not race and nature, as would become the case from the 1830s to the 1950s.[3]

The same Enlightenment ideas about human difference being based on culture are clear in the writings of the Royal Marine Watkin Tench, who recorded the British occupation of Eora Country in ethnographic detail. Tench, a veteran of the American War of Independence, referred to the Eora as the 'Indians.'[4] His writings, like those of Cook before him, were sympathetic towards Indigenous peoples. Tench's understanding of reality was clearly influenced by Rousseau's notions of human nature and the relationship between society and the natural world. For Tench, the 'Indians' of Port Jackson existed as living examples of the noble savage that Rousseau constructed in his philosophical imaginings. The influence of Enlightenment understandings of cultural diversity as an outcome of environmental contexts arguably reached its zenith under the colonial governorship of the Scot Lachlan Macquarie. Widely regarded by historians for the competence of his administration, Macquarie has recently become a figure of controversy for the part he played in sanctioning killings of Indigenous peoples while governor of New South Wales.[5] Despite the question marks that now hang over his legacy, the governorship of Macquarie provides perhaps the best examples of Enlightenment ideals intersecting and shaping colonial relations with Indigenous peoples. Macquarie's initiative to establish a school for the natives at Parramatta in 1814 stands as an education initiative that remained unsurpassed in education policy attitudes to Indigenous peoples until the post-1967 period.[6]

At a time before Australian governments had assumed responsibility for compulsory public schooling, Governor Macquarie built a school in which Aboriginal children could be formally educated and acculturated into British knowledge systems and 'civilisation.' Macquarie's School was built to test the central proposition of the Enlightenment – that native peoples could transition from a state of nature into civilisation through exposure to European education, social structures and norms.[7] In the government order establishing the School, Macquarie wrote that:

> to effect the Civilization of the Aborigines of New South Wales, and to render their Habits more domesticated and industrious His Excellency the Governor, as well from Motives of Humanity as of that Policy which afford a reasonable Hope of producing such an Improvement

Introduction 3

in their condition as may eventually contribute to render them not only more happy in themselves, but also in some Degree useful to the community.[8]

The idea that cultural difference was the result of environmental factors, such as geographic isolation, meant that processes of acculturation and assimilation became critical mechanisms to enact the Enlightenment in Australia. The Parramatta School is today remembered in Aboriginal education scholarship for being both a success and a failure. A female student of the School topped the Colony in an academic competition in 1819.[9] This outcome was used to suggest that acculturation and assimilation through education would ensure the natives of New South Wales would be civilised quickly, as they too collectively became enlightened. Yet such early successes proved short lived, as the parents of children sent to Macquarie's School began to question and resist the type of learning on offer.[10] As a result of growing Aboriginal resistance to a formal education that seemed irrelevant to Aboriginal cultural and economic needs, Macquarie's School was closed, and the Enlightenment ideas that inspired it ceased to direct colonial government policy in respect of the Aboriginal natives for the next 150 years.[11]

After the age of Macquarie, biological determinism – the belief that human behaviour is directly controlled by an individual's genes, or more broadly their physiology – became the ascendant theory of human diversity. Race replaced culture as the primary lens through which Europeans understood the rest of the world's humanity. The idea of a great chain of being first articulated by Aristotle in ancient Greece was applied in nineteenth-century Australia by settler colonists as a means to understand race relations on the frontier. This theory of race became highly influential at a time when land wars in New South Wales, sometimes known as the Bathurst Wars, were intensifying. Settler colonists often applied this race theory in ways that sought to deny the humanity of Aboriginal peoples. Regarded as the missing link between the animal kingdom and the races of man, Aboriginal peoples were often described as a species of tailless monkey by colonists hungry to dispossess Indigenous people of their Country.[12] The notion that human diversity was grounded in biological differences associated with race later became embedded in Social Darwinism, an intellectual movement that developed in the wake of Charles Darwin's publication of his theory of evolution in *On the Origin of Species* in 1859.[13] In the early decades of the twentieth century, Social Darwinism itself evolved into the dubious science of eugenics, through which characteristics that the nation considered deficit could be eradicated and erased by a state-sponsored program of selective breeding.[14] By the 1930s, human diversity had come to be understood primarily through this lens. Although most often associated with Nazi Germany,

4   *Barry Judd and Katherine Ellinghaus*

the science of eugenics was a dominant idea throughout the Western world during this period, and its ideas shaped native affairs policy across the British Empire from Canada to Australia, as well as in the United States of America. In Australia, eugenics, social Darwinism and biological conceptions of race – the conceptual framing of human difference that had led to the Holocaust – continued to exert influence over government policy and public perceptions of Indigenous peoples.[15] Only with the election of a national government led by Prime Minister E.G. Whitlam in the 1970s did more *enlightened* policies and attitudes return to centre stage, ones that focussed on culture and the possibility that Aboriginal people could be nurtured into the mainstream of contemporary Anglo-Australian society.

Enlightened Aboriginal Futures aims to shift the focus on Enlightenment thinking from Europe to Australia. This book is not a comprehensive description of every instance of Enlightenment thinking on this continent. Instead, we aim only to start a conversation that suggests the importance of broadening how we imagine the Enlightenment, both geographically and philosophically. In Australia, small pockets of believers in the ability of Aboriginal people to progress to 'civilisation' existed throughout the nineteenth and into the twentieth century. For example, in the 1830s British Quakers James Backhouse and George Washington Walker travelled to Van Diemen's Land, New South Wales and Swan River, pontificating humanitarian discourse and encouraging the antipodean governments to 'civilise' Aboriginal people.[16] In Victoria in the late nineteenth century, educated women such as Emily Stephen were taught, lauded and then targeted by Moravian missionaries and government officials who did not quite know what to do with them.[17] Moravian missionaries also orchestrated the mobility and publicised the marriages of other educated women, and baptised Wotjoballuk man Nathaniel Pepper who went on to preach at Ramayhuck in Gippsland.[18]

This book focuses on one of those pockets where Enlightenment ideas stood defiantly against the mainstream current of biological determinism – the work of Lutheran missionaries who travelled to Central Australia in the late nineteenth century. It explores the schemes they set up to educate Aranda, Luritja and other Anangu peoples that were designed to fuse German, Enlightenment values with those drawn from Aboriginal cultural traditions. Lutheran missionaries imported a number of key concepts to Central Australia that had their origins in eighteenth-century European Enlightenment thinking, and those ideas rubbed up against Aboriginal ideas of kinship, obligation and spirituality. In this book, we seek to add complexity not just to historical understandings of *where* Enlightenment thinking took place, but also to historical understandings of mission work in Australia. We examine the idea of mission work not only as oppressive and assimilationist, and instead recognise the ways this

Introduction 5

work could facilitate greater Indigenous freedom, choice and autonomy, often in opposition to the settler-colonial state and public opinion.

In adding such complexity to the history of assimilation in Australia, we examine it not just as a single set of oppressive policies, but as a multiplicity of relationships, ideas, programs and localised experiences. We also believe that assimilation was negotiated, and thus in some small ways shaped by the people who endured it. As historian Russell McGregor argued more than twenty years ago, to revisit the twentieth century in Australia – especially the middle third, seen as the heyday of assimilation – is to find

> that then 'assimilation' had no single meaning. It was a discourse which was informed by a diversity of intellectual currents and which produced significantly divergent visions of the Aboriginal destiny. Like all such discourses, assimilation was characterised as much by ambivalence and contention as by consistency and consensus. Appreciating the fact that assimilation was not unitary in meaning, nor necessarily totalising in outcome, may allow us to understand why, in the mid-twentieth century, it was attractive not only to politicians and other agents of the state but also to activists, humanitarians, churchmen, feminists and, not least, [Aboriginal people] themselves.[19]

In 1926, F. W. Albrecht arrived at Hermannsburg Mission in remote Central Australia from Germany. Steeped in Enlightenment ideas of reason, culture, nature and human diversity as well as being called to spread the word of God, he began working with the Aranda, Luritja and other Anangu peoples on whose Country Lutheran missionaries had settled to do their good works.[20] This book sees Albrecht's story not as remote or isolated, but as deeply linked to Enlightenment ideas. It asks how Albrecht's views on consent, freedom of choice and personal autonomy were expressed in a scheme designed to educate and empower Aboriginal people. The book then explores how Enlightenment ideas and Aboriginal epistemologies shaped the lives of the people with whom Albrecht worked and, more importantly, how Aboriginal people engaged with, created and utilised Enlightenment ideas (Figure I.1).

Albrecht's core idea that culture is more important than race and biology was never disrupted during his time in Central Australia. His thinking remained that of the eighteenth century more than that of the nineteenth, or that part of the twentieth that he himself lived and worked in. Despite the prevalence of pseudo-scientific ideas, Albrecht refused the logic of social Darwinism and did not accept the science of eugenics (despite the many visits to Ntaria/Hermannsburg from prominent people interested in the 'Aboriginal problem' who would have held these views). Rather, he imagined a future in which Aboriginal people would

Figure I.1 Pastor and Mrs F.W. Albrecht and family. Courtesy of the Lutheran Archives.

be part of the Australian community, contributing economically as equals to all other Australian citizens.[21] His sense of how to achieve this was vastly different from the thinking of settler-colonial government officials and assimilationists, and he rubbed up uncomfortably against the policies of the day, and, in particular, the officials and functionaries — from departmental secretaries to the social workers, school teachers and police forces — who enforced them.[22]

This book has four chapters. It begins with a sweeping, global analysis of the Enlightenment and Australia and finishes by drilling down into an educational scheme which involved, at its beginning, only a dozen or so people. We commence with a wide lens, exploring the history of the Enlightenment and its impact on the earliest years of invasion in Australia. We then examine how the Enlightenment was embodied in the work of missionary F. W. Albrecht at the Hermannsburg Mission in Central Australia. After that, we follow Albrecht to Mparntwe (Alice Springs) and trace just one part of his work in the early years of his (very active) retirement. We finish by examining the working of the education scheme that Albrecht facilitated and explore the way in which its origins in Enlightenment thinking made it so different from the ideas of the government of the day. We hear from one of the students who were involved and describe their one-on-one interactions with Albrecht. We give readers the

Introduction 7

flavour of this particular place and time through archival sources without, we hope, losing sight of the rich history, knowledge and cultures of Indigenous peoples in Australia that rarely finds itself recorded in the traditional historical record. And finally, we ask how this story might provide new insights and understandings to the complex issues and problems that confront contemporary Australian society today.

Beyond any text or academic engagement with the world lie the things that are normally hidden. Questions that concern the motivations of the authors to write about a particular topic and the origins of their interest are often deliberately obscured from the reader. Until recently, this has been the case in scholarly engagements in the sub-discipline of Australian history known euphemistically as Indigenous history. Perhaps because most of the scholars who claim to work in this field are themselves not Aboriginal, few have ventured into the realm of self-reflexivity. Yet this mode of academic enquiry has in recent years become emblematic and core to the field of Indigenous Studies in Australia and globally. As scholars who are deeply committed to building a better, more inclusive and equal Australia, we believe this work must start with self and aim to build better, more truthful relationships in the everyday through family and through work. As collaborating authors, our working relationship is perhaps an unusual one. On the surface of things, we share almost nothing in common and yet we do share a commitment to improving understanding of Australian race relations. We aim to do this through work that seeks to advocate on behalf of Aboriginal peoples in ways that acknowledge and pay respect and homage to the great antiquity of Indigenous life on this continent now called Australia. Our work references the challenge put to contemporary Australia by the prize-winning novelist Richard Flanagan. At the Garma Festival in 2018, Flanagan challenged Australians to confirm the two centuries plus engagement between Indigenous and non-Indigenous Australians as a relationship between kin. He did so by referencing the Yolngu concept of gurrutumiriw.[23] In our professional collaboration, we have taken the challenge set by Flanagan extremely seriously. It is a commitment that we believe must start with self-reflexivity and a willingness to tell the world where it is you are coming from.[24]

Barry Judd's contribution to this book is deeply entwined with his personal identity and Aboriginal heritage. Reflecting on the influence that Albrecht and his Lutheran and German ideas have exerted on his own life experience, Judd believes these to be many and complex. He admits that he has been assimilated into the Protestant work ethic and is over-concerned with tidiness, regimented order, routine and timeliness that comes with clock watching. Judd also admits to never fully understanding ANZAC Day or Anglo-Australian animosity to German Australians living here. German-Australian Lutherans had in his experience rejected the kind of ideas and actions the settler-state in Australia

8   *Barry Judd and Katherine Ellinghaus*

embraced, promoted and deployed against Indigenous peoples, and that in the 1930s-40s were deployed by the war machine of Adolf Hitler's Party of National Socialism in Europe against the, Jews, Gypsies, Slavs, the disabled and gender diverse. Judd thinks Aimé Césaire was right when he said the only crime of National Socialism was to force the inhumanity, death and despair of colonial logic upon Europe.[25] This is an insight, he believes, that the average Anglo-Australian on ANZAC Day (and Australia Day) continues to conveniently overlook. Then there is Judd's commitment to formal education as something capable of transforming and enriching the lives of individuals and communities, grounded perhaps in Lutheranism and the need to read. A major thread in his academic research has been the study of the new and transformative identity formations that emerge in settler-colonial contexts as each side of the settler and native divide is transformed through agency, freedom of choice and the exercise of political autonomy.[26] On reflection, his research interest in the development of the cultural hybrid and a belief that the identity formations that arise in colonial/post-colonial contests are countless and largely indeterminable — as well as a manifest rejection of the binaries proposed by the nationalism of the political right and the essentialisms of the political left — could likely be traced back to the interventions of Albrecht and his German Enlightenment ideas about the centrality of culture in shaping and transforming (Aboriginal) identity in Judd's own family.

Through his research (including this collaboration with Katherine Ellinghaus), Judd has been able to work with family and kin as knowledge holders of law and culture in their efforts to create better futures – futures that will continue to be shaped by the *Volkgeist* of the Pitjantjatjara/Luritja/Aranda-Arrernte of Central Australia. It is work that has confirmed many of the beneficial outcomes that have arisen from the Finke River Mission intervention in formal Western education. Judd remembers an exchange that took place early in his research work at Papunya. Sitting by a campfire, his kin brother, who also acted as key informant to the research, was overheard responding to another senior man in Luritja. His brother's response in English approximates to 'What's wrong? Don't you have a family who are whitefellas like him too?' Judd remains grateful to his grandmother and uncle for the consent and support they provided his mother and is indebted to Albrecht and those German-Australian Lutherans whose support of his scheme made her formal Western education and the intergenerational life opportunities and choices that have resulted possible. He continues to hold those who helped his mother receive a quality formal Western education in high regard. If not for them, it is possible to speculate that Judd would not have become Professor of Indigenous Studies at the University of Melbourne (Figure I.2).

Figure I.2 'In the schoolroom at Hermannsburg.' Courtesy of the Lutheran Archives.

The interest in writing this book for Katherine Ellinghaus is similarly reflective of personal identity and cultural heritage. The child of a German immigrant and a third-generation Irish/Scottish/German Australian, Ellinghaus was raised without learning the German language and with little interaction with German culture. In March 1955, the *Anna Salen*, the ship carrying her father and his two brothers, together with their parents (as well as his maternal grandmother), docked at Melbourne. Having made the decision to flee the political uncertainty and financial hardships of post-war Germany her grandparents and their sons were part of 1.3 million migrants who entered Australia between 1947 and 1961. Whether her family was also fleeing any memory of or collusion in the many crimes that became a Holocaust in Poland and Germany between 1933 and 1945 was almost never discussed. They settled in the Victorian Country town of Seymour, where her grandmother's sister and her husband, previous immigrants, had established a café and bought the small house in which they would live for the rest of their lives. The family encountered significant anti-German sentiment: Ellinghaus' grandfather, despite his engineering qualifications and managerial record, was only able to find work as a weaver in a factory. Her father was greeted on his first day at school with a water pistol filled with urine. The extent to which the pressure to conform to Anglo-Australian culture was resisted by her immigrant parent and his grandparents is still unclear to

10 *Barry Judd and Katherine Ellinghaus*

her, but it certainly influenced a childhood in which she grew up feeling not quite like the majority of the other children in the school playground. But Ellinghaus also felt disconnected to the German branch of her family, as though the long voyage on the *Anna Salen* had severed some strand of her identity. This was, apparently, not uncommon in German families in the post-war period. Gabriele Rosenthal's 1998 collection of family stories based on interviews with three generations of both Holocaust survivors and perpetrators shows in dispassionate sociological terms that children of the latter often know very little about their own family histories. It is, Rosenthal intimates, a form of denial. Still, Ellinghaus feels, like Judd, deeply disconnected from nationalistic celebrations of ANZAC or World War II diggers. It dawned on her in her childhood that her grandfather's service as an officer in the German Army was not something to celebrate on ANZAC day. She later researched her family history and began to think about the two attempted genocides to which she is connected through her family histories – one in Europe, one on the Australian continent. The past was no longer a place of heroes and villains. She began to see that one of the impacts of post-war assimilation schemes was not simply a diversification of the population and a strengthening of the economy, but also the arrival of immigrants whose children might be disconnected both from their own family history and that of settler-colonial Australia.

Thus Ellinghaus understands, in the absence of any kinship with the Lutherans who made their way to Central Australia in the 1870s, how their outsider whiteness might have enabled them to view Aboriginal people's futures in ways that differed markedly from mainstream Anglo-Australian perceptions. Judd was also, he jokes, raised by Germans. Their shared German connections have led Judd and Ellinghaus to wonder whether this factor plays a significant part in their collaboration. Both were imbued in their childhoods with a deep respect for higher education and German values of hard work, efficiency and high levels of 'achievement'. But more than this, both share a deep scepticism and suspicion of race-based forms of Anglo-Australian nationalism.

This introduction, we hope, sets the stage for what follows and why we as authors think new explorations and assessments of the European Enlightenment that are grounded in an Australian context are of critical importance in efforts to understand contemporary Australian politics and society. The story of F. W. Albrecht and the work he undertook in the name of the Lutheran Finke River Mission in Central Australia during the mid-twentieth century provides an exemplary case study of how the central ideas of the Enlightenment became known to the Aboriginal peoples of the central and western desert regions and how they often responded positively to the ideas Albrecht had brought with him from far away Germany.

Introduction 11

Notes

1 For scholarship which examines the Enlightenment in the Australian context, see Alan Atkinson, *The Europeans in Australia: A History*, Vol. 1 (Melbourne: Oxford University Press, 1997); Manning Clark, *A History of Australia*, Vol. 1 (Carlton: Melbourne University Press, 1962); Manning Clark, 'Some Influences of European Civilisation on Australia,' *Papers and Proceedings*, Tasmanian Historical Research Association 7, No. 2 (1958): 19–25; Robert Dixon, *The Course of Empire: Neo-Classical Culture in New South Wales 1788–1860* (Melbourne: Oxford University Press, 1986); John Gascoigne, *The Enlightenment and the Origins of European Australia* (Port Melbourne, VIC: Cambridge University Press, 2002); Jan Kociumbas, *Oxford History of Australia*, Vol. 2, 1770–1890 (Melbourne: Oxford University Press, 1995); Shino Konishi, *The Aboriginal Male in the Enlightenment World* (London: Pickering and Chatto, 2012); Austin Lovegrove, *Images of the Australian Enlightenment: The Story of Lachlan and Elizabeth Macquarie's Treatment of the Convicts* (London: Unicorn Press, 2019); Greg Melleuish, *Cultural Liberalism in Australia: A Study in Intellectual and Cultural History* (Cambridge: Cambridge University Press, 1995); Benjamin Wilkie, 'Scotland's Enlightenment in Australia: Scottish Moral and Political Thought from Macquarie to Menzies,' *Journal of the Sydney Society for Scottish History* 19 (2021): 17–30.
2 B. Bailyn, *The Ideological Origins of the American Revolution* (Cambridge, MA: Harvard University Press, 1967); H. Commager, *The Empire of Reason: How Europe Imagined and America Realised the Enlightenment* (New York: Anchor Press, 1977); Jonathan Israel, *Democratic Enlightenment: Philosophy, Revolution, and Human Rights 1750–1790* (Oxford: Oxford University Press, 2013); Roy Porter and Mikulas Teich, eds., *The Enlightenment in National Context* (Cambridge, New York: Cambridge University Press, 1981).
3 Gascoigne, *The Enlightenment and the Origins of European Australia*, 12–13.
4 Watkins Tench, *A Narrative of the Expedition to Botany Bay; With an Account of New South Wales, Its Productions, Inhabitants, &c. To Which Is Subjoined, a List of the Civil and Military Establishments at Port Jackson* (London: Printed for J. Debrett, n.d. [1789]).
5 For example, R. Howitt, L. Holt and M. L. Locke, 'Challenging the Colonial Legacy of/at Macquarie,' *Geographical Research* 60, No. 1 (2022): 71–85. https://doi.org/10.1111/1745-5871.12496.
6 See J. Brook and J. L. Kohen, *The Parramatta Native Institution and the Black Town: A History* (Kensington, NSW: New South Wales University Press, 1991).
7 On the establishment of the institution, see J. Fletcher, *Clean, Clad and Courteous: A History of Aboriginal Education in New South Wales* (Carlton, NSW: J. Fletcher, 1989), 19–22.
8 'Establishment of the Native Institution, 1814 – Government and General Order,' NRS 1046 [SZ759, pages 11–14; Reel 6038], State Records Office of New South Wales, https://www.records.nsw.gov.au/sites/default/files/Galleries/Lachlan%20Macquarie/native-institution.pdf, accessed 11 February 2022.
9 Jack Brook, 'Lock, Maria,' in *Dictionary of Sydney* (2008) http://dictionaryofsydney.org/entry/lock_maria, accessed 27 Jan 2023; J. Brook and J. L. Kohen, 'The Lock Family,' in *The Parramatta Native Institution and the Black Town: A History* (Kensington, NSW: New South Wales University Press, 1991), 249–259.
10 Brook and Kohen, *The Parramatta Native Institution and the Black Town*, 262–263, 267; Rosemary Norman-Hill, 'Australia's Native Residential Schools,'

12   Barry Judd and Katherine Ellinghaus

in *Residential Schools and Indigenous Peoples: From Genocide via Education to the Possibilities for Processes of Truth, Restitution, Reconciliation, and Reclamation* ed. Stephen Minton (London: Routledge, 2019).

11 John Locke, *An Essay Concerning Human Understanding* (Oxford, NY: Oxford University Press, 1690).

12 Henry Reynolds, *Frontier: Aborigines, Settlers and Land* (St Leonards, NSW: Allen and Unwin, 1996).

13 Charles Darwin, *The Origin of Species by Means of Natural Selection, or the Preservation of Favoured Races in the Struggle for Life* (Cambridge: Cambridge University Press, 2009).

14 Stephen Garton, 'Sound Minds and Healthy Bodies: Re-considering Eugenics in Australia, 1914–1940,' *Australian Historical Studies* 26, No. 103 (1995): 161–181.

15 Stephen Garton, 'Eugenics in Australia and New Zealand: Laboratories of Racial Science,' in *The Oxford Handbook of the History of Eugenics*, eds. Alison Bashford and Philippa Levine (Oxford, NY: Oxford University Press, 2010), 243–257. https://doi.org/10.1093/oxfordhb/9780195373141.013.0014; Anna Haebich, *Broken Circles: Fragmenting Indigenous Families 1800–2000* (Fremantle, WA: Fremantle Arts Centre Press, 2000), 271–276.

16 Penelope Edmonds, 'Travelling "Under Concern": Quakers James Backhouse and George Washington Walker Tour the Antipodean Colonies, 1832–41,' *Journal of Imperial and Commonwealth History* 40, No. 5 (December 2012): 769–788.

17 Patricia Grimshaw and Elizabeth Nelson, 'Empire, "the Civilising Mission" and Indigenous Christian Women in Colonial Victoria,' *Australian Feminist Studies* 16, No. 36 (2001): 296–297.

18 Jane Lydon and Alan Burns, 'Memories of the Past, Visions of the Future: Changing Views of Ebenezer Mission, Victoria, Australia,' *International Journal of Historical Archaeology* 14, No. 1 (March 2010): 39–55; Felicity Jensz, 'Controlling Marriages: Friedrich Hagenauer and the Betrothal of Indigenous Western Australian Women in Colonial Victoria,' *Aboriginal History* 34 (2010): 35–54.

19 Russell McGregor, 'Wards, Words and Citizens: A.P. Elkin and Paul Hasluck on Assimilation,' *Oceania* 69, No. 4 (1999): 244–245.

20 For discussion of how God 'survived' the Enlightenment, see William J. Bulman and Robert G. Ingram, eds., *God in the Enlightenment* (New York, 2016; online edition, Oxford Academic, 23 June 2016).

21 Barbara Henson, *A Straight-Out Man: F.W. Albrecht and Central Australian Aborigines* (Parkville, VIC: Melbourne University Press, 1992), 227.

22 For example, see Henson, *A Straight-Out Man*, 134–153.

23 Flanagan argued that '[i]n Yolngu the word for selfish is gurrutumiriw, which translates as lacking in kin, or acting as if one has no kin... Black and white, we have become kin. We cannot be selfish.' Richard Flanagan, 'Garma Festival Speech,' (Speech Transcript, Gulkula, 6 August 2018), https://www.cread.com.au/2018/08/author-richard-flanagans-speech-to.html, accessed 2 December 2022.

24 The authors of this book have written about their collaboration and the 'wicked problem' of the discipline of history that it seeks to address. See Katherine Ellinghaus and Barry Judd, 'Writing as Kin: F. W. Albrecht, Assimilation Policy and the Lutheran experiment in Aboriginal Education, 1950s–1960s,' in *Indigenous-Settler Relations in Australia and the World*, eds. Sarah Maddison and Sana Nakata (Singapore: Springer Nature, 2020), 55–68, Barry Judd and Katherine Ellinghaus, 'F. W. Albrecht, Assimilation Policy and the Education

of Aboriginal Girls in Central Australia: Overcoming Disciplinary Decadence in Australian History,' *Journal of Australian Studies* 44, No. 2 (April 2020): 167–181, and Katherine Ellinghaus and Barry Judd, 'The Spirit of Place: Overcoming the Fear of Authentic Indigenous Engagements in Australian History,' photo essay for inclusion in *Memory in Place: Locating History and Commemoration*, eds. Cameo Dalley and Ash Barnwell, proposal for collection submitted to ANU Press (forthcoming 2023).

25 Aimé Césaire and Joan Pinkham, *Discourse on Colonialism* (online, NYU Press, 2000), http://www.jstor.org/stable/j.ctt9qfkrm.

26 Barry Judd, Lynette Russell and Sarah J. Pritchard, 'Australian Game, Australian Identity: (Post) colonial Identity in Football' (PhD Thesis: Monash University Publishing, 2007). See also Joel Liddle and Barry Judd, 'Altyerre NOW: Arrernte Dreams for National Reconstruction in the 21st Century,' *Learning Communities: International Journal of Learning in Social Contexts* 23 (2018): 106–111; Jesse Fleay and Barry Judd, 'The Uluru Statement: A First Nations Perspective of the Implications for Social Reconstructive Race Relations in Australia,' *International Journal of Critical Indigenous Studies* 12, No. 1 (2019): 1–14.

Bibliography

Primary

'Establishment of the Native Institution, 1814 – Government and General Order,' NRS 1046 [SZ759, pages 11–14; Reel 6038]. State Records Office of New South Wales, https://www.records.nsw.gov.au/sites/default/files/Galleries/Lachlan%20Macquarie/native-institution.pdf, accessed 11 February 2022.

Flanagan, Richard. 'Garma Festival Speech.' Speech Transcript, Gulkula, 6 August 2018, https://www.cread.com.au/2018/08/author-richard-flanagans-speech-to.html, accessed 2 December 2022.

Tench, Watkins. *A Narrative of the Expedition to Botany Bay; with an Account of New South Wales, Its Productions, Inhabitants, &c. To Which Is Subjoined, a List of the Civil and Military Establishments at Port Jackson*. London: Printed for J. Debrett, n.d. [1789].

Secondary

Atkinson, Alan. *The Europeans in Australia: A History*, Volume 1. Melbourne: Oxford University Press, 1997.

Bailyn, B. *The Ideological Origins of the American Revolution*. Cambridge, MA: Harvard University Press, 1967.

Brook, J. 'Lock, Maria,' in *Dictionary of Sydney* (2008) http://dictionaryofsydney.org/entry/lock_maria, accessed 27 Jan 2023.

Brook, J and J. L. Kohen. *The Parramatta Native Institution and the Black Town: A History*. Kensington, NSW: New South Wales University Press, 1991.

Bulman, William J. and Robert G. Ingram, editors. *God in the Enlightenment*. New York, 2016; online edition, Oxford Academic, 23 June 2016.

Césaire, Aimé and Joan Pinkham. *Discourse on Colonialism*. Online, NYU Press, 2000. http://www.jstor.org/stable/j.ctt9qfkrm.

14 *Barry Judd and Katherine Ellinghaus*

Clark, Manning. *A History of Australia*, Volume 1. Carlton: Melbourne University Press, 1962.

Clark, Manning. 'Some influences of European civilisation on Australia.' *Papers and Proceedings*, Tasmanian Historical Research Association 7, Number 2 (1958): 19–25.

Commager, H. *The Empire of Reason: How Europe imagined and America realised the Enlightenment*. New York: Anchor Press, 1977.

Darwin, Charles. *The Origin of Species by Means of Natural Selection, or the Preservation of Favoured Races in the Struggle for Life*. Cambridge: Cambridge University Press, 2009.

Dixon, Robert. *The Course of Empire: Neo-Classical Culture in New South Wales 1788–1860*. Melbourne: Oxford University Press, 1986.

Edmonds, Penelope. 'Travelling "Under Concern": Quakers James Backhouse and George Washington Walker Tour the Antipodean Colonies, 1832–41.' *Journal of Imperial and Commonwealth History* 40, Number 5 (December 2012): 769–788.

Ellinghaus, Katherine and Barry Judd. 'The Spirit of Place: Overcoming the fear of authentic Indigenous engagements in Australian history.' Photo essay for inclusion in *Memory in Place: Locating History and Commemoration*, edited by Cameo Dalley and Ash Barnwell, proposal for collection submitted to ANU Press (forthcoming 2023).

Ellinghaus, Katherine and Barry Judd. 'Writing as Kin: F. W. Albrecht, Assimilation Policy and the Lutheran experiment in Aboriginal Education, 1950s–1960s.' In *Indigenous-Settler Relations in Australia and the World,* edited by Sarah Maddison and Sana Nakata. Singapore: Springer Nature, 2020.

Fleay, Jesse and Barry Judd. 'The Uluru Statement: A First Nations Perspective of the Implications for Social Reconstructive Race Relations in Australia.' *International Journal of Critical Indigenous Studies* 12, Number 1 (2019): 1–14.

Fletcher, J. *Clean, Clad and Courteous: A History of Aboriginal Education in New South Wales*. Carlton, NSW: J. Fletcher, 1989.

Garton, Stephen. 'Eugenics in Australia and New Zealand: Laboratories of Racial Science.' In *The Oxford Handbook of the History of Eugenics,* edited by Alison Bashford and Philippa Levine. Oxford, NY: Oxford University Press, 2010, 243–257. https://doi.org/10.1093/oxfordhb/9780195373141.013.0014.

Garton, Stephen. 'Sound Minds and Healthy Bodies: Re-considering Eugenics in Australia, 1914–1940.' *Australian Historical Studies* 26, Number 103 (1995): 161–181.

Gascoigne, John. *The Enlightenment and the Origins of European Australia*. Port Melbourne, VIC: Cambridge University Press, 2002.

Grimshaw, Patricia and Elizabeth Nelson. 'Empire, "the Civilising Mission" and Indigenous Christian Women in Colonial Victoria.' *Australian Feminist Studies* 16, Number 36 (2001): 295–309.

Haebich, Anna. *Broken Circles: Fragmenting Indigenous Families 1800–2000*. Fremantle, WA: Fremantle Arts Centre Press, 2000.

Henson, Barbara. *A Straight-Out Man: F.W. Albrecht and Central Australian Aborigines*. Parkville, VIC: Melbourne University Press, 1992.

Howitt, R, L. Holt and M. L. Locke, 'Challenging the colonial legacy of/at Macquarie.' *Geographical Research* 60, Number 1 (2022): 71–85. https://doi.org/10.1111/1745-5871.12496.

Introduction 15

Israel, Jonathan. *Democratic Enlightenment: Philosophy, Revolution, and Human Rights 1750–1790.* Oxford: Oxford University Press, 2013.

Jensz, Felicity. 'Controlling Marriages: Friedrich Hagenauer and the betrothal of Indigenous Western Australian women in colonial Victoria.' *Aboriginal History* 34 (2010): 35–54.

Judd, Barry and Katherine Ellinghaus. 'F. W. Albrecht, Assimilation Policy and the Education of Aboriginal girls in Central Australia: Overcoming Disciplinary Decadence in Australian History.' *Journal of Australian Studies* 44, Number 2 (April 2020): 167–181.

Judd, Barry, Lynette Russell and S. J. Pritchard. 'Australian Game, Australian Identity: (Post) Colonial identity in football.' PhD Thesis: Monash University Publishing, 2007.

Kociumbas, Jan. *Oxford History of Australia,* Volume 2, 1770–1890. Melbourne: Oxford University Press, 1995.

Konishi, Shino. *The Aboriginal Male in the Enlightenment World.* London: Pickering and Chatto, 2012.

Liddle, Joel and Barry Judd. 'Altyerre NOW: Arrernte Dreams for National Reconstruction in the 21st Century.' *Learning Communities: International Journal of Learning in Social Contexts* 23 (2018): 106–111.

Locke, John. *An Essay Concerning Human Understanding.* Oxford, NY: Oxford University Press, 1690.

Lovegrove, Austin. *Images of the Australian Enlightenment: The Story of Lachlan and Elizabeth Macquarie's Treatment of the Convicts.* London: Unicorn Press, 2019.

Lydon, Jane and Alan Burns. 'Memories of the Past, Visions of the Future: Changing Views of Ebenezer Mission, Victoria, Australia.' *International Journal of Historical Archaeology* 14, Number 1 (March 2010): 39–55.

McGregor, Russell. 'Wards, Words and Citizens: A. P. Elkin and Paul Hasluck on Assimilation.' *Oceania* 69, Number 4 (1999): 243–259.

Melleuish, Greg. *Cultural Liberalism in Australia: A Study in Intellectual and Cultural History.* Cambridge: Cambridge University Press, 1995.

Norman-Hill, Rosemary. 'Australia's Native Residential Schools.' In *Residential Schools and Indigenous Peoples: From Genocide via Education to the Possibilities for Processes of Truth, Restitution, Reconciliation, and Reclamation,* edited by Stephen Minton. London: Routledge, 2019.

Porter, Ray and Mikulas Teich, editors. *The Enlightenment in National Context.* Cambridge, New York: Cambridge University Press, 1981.

Reynolds, Henry. *Frontier: Aborigines, Settlers and Land.* St Leonards, NSW: Allen and Unwin, 1996.

Rosenthal, Gabriele. 'Similarities and Differences in Family Dialog.' In *The Holocaust in Three Generations: Families of Victims and Perpetrators of the Nazi Regime* edited by Gabriele Rosenthal. London: Cassell, 1998.

Wilkie, Benjamin. 'Scotland's Enlightenment in Australia: Scottish Moral and Political Thought from Macquarie to Menzies.' *Journal of the Sydney Society for Scottish History,* 19 (2021): 17–30.

1 Made in Germany
The Import of Lutheranism and Enlightenment in Central Australia

Barry Judd

In the aftermath of the Stolen Generations and national recognition of the trauma caused by past policies and practices that authorised the forced removal of Aboriginal children from their families, the history of Christian missions in Australia has been increasingly assessed in negative terms.[1] Missions and the work of Christian missionaries have become so entangled with the issue of the Stolen Generations that the historical legacy of their work has become overwhelmingly associated with the destruction of Aboriginal families, cultures, religion, languages and connections to Country. As a result, few contemporary Australian historians who write 'Aboriginal history' explore the history of missions in ways that move beyond the lens of settler-colonial studies. Instead, simplistic divisions of good and evil are too often used in contemporary historical analysis of past relations between settler-colonists and indigenous peoples.[2] Our research about the history of Lutheran missions in Central Australia was in large part inspired by the eminent Australian history Geoffrey Blainey who, during a public talk Judd attended over a decade ago, responded to a question from the public about the role of Church and mission in the propagation of the Stolen Generations.[3] Blainey advised his audience of the dangers of generalising when considering the historical work of Church and mission in their interactions with Aboriginal Australia. As an example, he referenced the work of the Lutheran Church and their Finke River Mission at Hermannsburg in the Central Australian region of the Northern Territory as an exemplary case where the historical work of missions and the emergence of the Stolen Generations constitute two very separate and distinctive stories in Australian history. In saying this, Blainey bemoaned the fact that no contemporary historians in Australia seemed interested in researching the Lutherans at Hermannsburg as a counter narrative to the politically fashionable story that missions everywhere were directly responsible for the Stolen Generations and the destruction of Aboriginal culture and society.[4]

DOI: 10.4324/9781003281634-2

Made in Germany 17

Our work is an attempt to deliberately complicate these histories in ways that meet the challenge set by Blainey. In doing so, we seek to disrupt theories of settler-colonialism that now dominate Indigenous Studies and 'Aboriginal history.' The structuralist approach to history implicit in settler-colonial theory draws a picture of the Australian past where settlers' insatiable greed for land drive them to eliminate the Aboriginal natives. While the theory has been undoubtedly useful, the danger in this framing is that the Aboriginal natives are portrayed as helpless victims of the economic machine of settler-colonialism who resign themselves to their own mass destruction, acting as mindless lemmings jumping in the abyss. Our writings about Lutheran missions are instead consistent with recent critiques of settler-colonialism theory and the historical understandings that emerge from it.[5]

Building on such previous work, this chapter is written in part to bring new complications to the story of Church missions in Australia and the ways these Christian initiatives interacted with Aboriginal peoples. More than this, this chapter retraces the story of how German- and Polish-speaking Lutherans from the Kingdom of Prussia came to settle and form their distinctive communities in the newly established British colony of South Australia from 1838. It explores why, as cultural, linguistic and religious outsiders to British settler-colonialism, they felt compelled to engage with the Aboriginal peoples of the colony through mission.[6] In retracing this history, we argue that one important consequence of Lutheran engagements with Aboriginal peoples has been the transfer of ideas and values from Europe to Australia. It is our argument that the mission men from Prussia and their wives did not just take bibles, cattle and sheep to Central Australia, but they also carried with them the central ideas of the Enlightenment. These ideas, we contend, came to shape the ongoing relationship between Lutherans and the Aboriginal peoples they worked with in Central Australia through their Finke River Mission, established at Hermannsburg in 1878. As this relationship matured in the middle decades of the twentieth century, we argue that Enlightenment ideals were applied in particular by head missionary F. W. Albrecht as tools designed to find possible social, political and economic futures for the Western Aranda and other Aboriginal peoples in Central Australia.[7] Under the direction of Albrecht, initiatives in formal education and capitalist economics were used to instil Enlightenment ideals about the importance of duty and of personal responsibility, knowledge underpinned by the logic of rationalism and scientific principle and the importance of work ethic to successful private enterprise and financial independence.[8]

Albrecht, a product of German culture, had a commitment to Aboriginal futures because he viewed culture as more important than race and understood that Aboriginal progress would take place through a process

18 *Barry Judd*

of social and economic integration into the national community and the global economic system. His belief in the primacy of culture, cultural relativism and progress through historicised reason were ideas that framed his work with Aboriginal peoples that owed much more to the age of German Enlightenment (and his commitment to Lutheran theological teachings) than it did to the settler-colonial race polices of twentieth-century Anglo-Australia.

Although we have come to understand the work undertaken by Lutheran missions in Australia to be an outcome of the import of Enlightenment ideas into the continent now known as Australia, most academic writings and institutional understanding of the Enlightenment continue to frame the period as something that emerged in Europe and whose impacts, concerns and consequences continue to be primarily European ones. The history of the Enlightenment is often seen as the history of French, German and Scottish ideas that are discussed and critiqued in a quite disconnected way from the development of European colonial empire with few notable exceptions writing from the margins the philosophical mainstream.[9] Such a view of the Enlightenment risks masking the entanglement between the central ideas of the Enlightenment and the development of colonial and imperial governance as their substantive outcome. This approach also risks ignoring the fact that the Enlightenment was financially underwritten by the enormous wealth that came from colonial empire and its active involvement in the transatlantic slave trade, and the dispossession of indigenous peoples in a global process of economic exploitation and human suffering.[10] One of the most critical points to emerge from our work on Albrecht and the Lutheran mission in Central Australia is that settlers from Britain and elsewhere and the Aboriginal peoples they encountered and formed relationships with became participants in a world shaped by Enlightenment ideas and values, and their material consequences in politics, society and economics. As a study of the application of Enlightenment ideals in the context of Australian settler-colonialism, our writing is necessarily characterised by messiness, ambivalence and stark contradictions. This is because we are exploring a philosophical approach that emphasised liberty, equality and fraternity and rested on the cornerstone of reason against the historical backdrop of settler-colonialism – a process which was driven by the imperative of eliminating Indigenous peoples and cultures and obliterating their memory. The neatness of studying the Enlightenment as a philosophical movement in the confines of Europe therefore evaporates when the view turns to the places possessed by European colonialism and exploited by European imperialism. This fact not only becomes obvious when assessing the consequences of colonialism and imperialism as broad historical processes that are global in scale and impact, but also in the study of localised histories that are specific to time, place and the local

Made in Germany 19

communities, institutions and individuals whose agency shaped things in the past, including relations between settler-colonists and Indigenous peoples.

Our study of Lutheran mission in Central Australia seeks to remind contemporary Australians that in some cases the work of missionaries was motivated more by the philosophical ideals embodied in the Enlightenment than they were by the imperatives of British and Anglo-Australian settler-colonialism and empire. Nonetheless, the former and the latter remain highly entangled and are impossible to separate. The missionary work of F. W. Albrecht in Central Australia, while primarily shaped by Enlightenment ideals of personal autonomy and the potential of all human beings for self-improvement through education and hard work, was tempered by his many entanglements with the apparatus of power that enforced settler-colonial law and order over the Western Aranda and other Aboriginal peoples in Central Australia. For example, in the early 1930s, on the advice of Albrecht, policeman Constable William McKinnon commissioned several poker stick drawings on wood by the emergent Western Aranda artist and Hermannsburg resident Albert Namatjira.[11] The drawings by Namatjira depicted McKinnon on camel patrolling the southwest region of the Northern Territory, Country occupied by Luritja, Yankuntjatjarra and Pitjantjatjara peoples. On one of these patrols in 1934, McKinnon shot and killed a Yankuntjatjarra-Pitjantjatjara man at Mutitjulu Waterhole at the base of Uluru.[12] In this small and perhaps insignificant way, Albrecht becomes implicated in the memory of frontier violence and the settler-colonial drive to eliminate Indigenous peoples that occurred in Central Australia from the 1870s – and that arguably continues, transformed but unrelenting, to the present day. And although Albrecht opposed the policy of forced removal of Aboriginal children, McKinnon – the policeman who was responsible for carrying out this policy by stealing children away from their mothers – sometimes sought the company and conversation of Albrecht as a fellow white man on the isolated frontier as much as he sought refuge and respite from the unrelenting harshness of the central desert at the Lutheran mission at Hermannsburg. That Albrecht [Figure 1.1], the man whose life work was informed by Enlightenment ideals, knew McKinnon, the man whose life work was to facilitate settler-colonialism through the elimination of Indigenous people, and existed in the same historical time and place demonstrates the extent to which notions such as liberty, autonomy, equality, fraternity and reasons coexisted and competed alongside ideas such as scientific racism, dying race theory, breeding out the colour, segregation, assimilation and absorption. The complications and entanglements of ideas and the people who advocated and actioned as well as opposed Enlightenment ideas on the Central Australian frontier that unfolded in the context of global imperialism and settler-colonialism

Figure 1.1 'Maryvale, NT, Finke River Mission Rev FW Albrecht, right, distributing rations of dried fruit, peas etc. to local people for cash sales at reasonable prices.' Courtesy of the Lutheran Archives.

stand in stark contrast to the lives of the key philosophers who originated the Enlightenment. For example, the Prussian philosopher Immanuel Kant whose ethical framework drew on Lutheran understanding of duty never travelled more than a few miles beyond the confines of his home city of Königsberg.[13]

Religious Asylum Seekers: The Coming of Old Lutheran Mission to Colonial South Australia

As the first Protestant Church of the Reformation, the Lutherans became the dominant organised religion in northern Germany and the Nordic countries of Europe and quickly established themselves as the state religions of Prussia, Denmark and Sweden. In the nineteenth century, the Prussian King Frederick William III enacted several royal decrees designed to unify the Protestant Churches of his kingdom. These decrees led to the unification of the Lutheran and Reformed denomination in 1817, under what is commonly referred to as the Prussian Union.[14] The Union of these Protestant Churches was the culmination of a process that the King had commenced in 1799, with the introduction of a common liturgical agenda or service book to be used by pastors in both the Lutheran and

Made in Germany 21

Reformed Churches. The King's attempts to direct and control the ways in which Lutheran congregations would now commune with God were not universally accepted. Significant sections of the Lutheran Church in Prussia, and particularly in the Province of Silesia, resisted what they took to be the unwelcome intrusion of state power into matters that concerned God and Church. The resistance was led by Johann Gottfried Scheibel (1783–1843) and those who followed him became commonly known as the 'Old Lutherans'. By the 1830s, Old Lutheran resistance to what they believed to be a gross misuse of state power led many to seek religious freedoms beyond the control of the Prussian King. Some of these Old Lutherans decided that the best place to practice their religion free from state interference was in the United States of America.[15] Thousands settled in the Midwest and Upper Midwest of the United States of America during this period.

At the same time, another group of Old Lutherans left their homelands to find religious freedom in the newly established British colony of South Australia. In 1838 four ships – the *Prince George, Bengalee, Zebra* and *Catharina* – arrived in South Australia. The most important group of Old Lutherans arrived on the barque *Bengalee* at Port Adelaide on 16 November 1838. On board were 33 passengers. They were led by Pastor August Ludwig Christian Kavel.[16] Kavel is today widely recognised as the father of Lutheranism in Australia. Under his leadership Klemzig (now a suburb of Adelaide) was established as the first Old Lutheran settlement in South Australia. As more ships arrived, the Old Lutherans in South Australia soon established other settlement – at Glen Osmond and Hahndorf. A community of farming people, they later expanded their settlements beyond Adelaide and its surrounding hills. In the 1840s, they took up land in the Barossa Valley northeast of Adelaide and established South Australia as a major wine producer and added much to its agricultural output. From the now well-established community in South Australia, Old Lutherans undertook intercolonial migrations with new farming communities from the 1850s to the 1870s, including those established in the Wimmera region of Victoria and the Southern Riverina region of New South Wales.[17]

The Old Lutherans who found religious sanctuary in the British possession of South Australia did so with the authority of Queen Victoria and with the financial assistance of George Fife Angas.[18] Angas and his South Australian Company met significant transport costs via generous loans for the ships to South Australia. Although Fife Angas, like many of the British merchant class of the time, had inherited much of the family wealth through the West Indian sugar trade and was therefore implicated in the consequences of slavery, he insisted the colony of South Australia adopt a protectionist policy with respect to Aboriginal peoples. From the very beginnings of the Old Lutheran settlements in South Australia, a concern

22 *Barry Judd*

for the welfare of the native peoples was evident. Among the very first of the Old Lutheran immigrants to arrive in South Australia were Clamor Wilhelm Schürmann and Christian Gottlieb Teichelmann. They landed in Adelaide in October 1838, one month before Pastor Kavel. These were men who had committed themselves to opening an engagement with the Aboriginal 'natives'.[19] Upon their arrival, Schürmann and Teichelmann commenced Lutheran mission with the Aboriginal peoples of the Colony. Their mission to the Bangarla and Kaurna peoples is remembered for the significant work the pair took in the documentation of these Aboriginal Australian languages. In the twenty-first century, their commitment to learn, record and translate these languages plays an important part in their present-day reconstruction and revival.[20] Significantly for a book that is focussed on the import and currency of Enlightenment ideas in settler-colonial Australia, Schürmann and Teichelmann are also remembered for a school they founded for Kaurna people at Piltawodli in the Adelaide parklands. Their focus on the local vernacular and on formal education set the template for later missions to the Aborigines that Old Lutherans in Australia would commit to.[21]

Building on the experience of Schürmann and Teichelmann, the Old Lutherans' community in the Barossa Valley backed a new mission to the Aborigines in the arid interior of South Australia.[22] Beyond their farms and the agriculture of the settled districts, as proclaimed by Goyder's Line, lay the desert Country of the outback. This was a place yet unconquered by settler-colonists and one which remained largely under the control of Indigenous peoples. In 1866, into the unsettled districts of the arid interior the Old Lutherans of South Australia sent the missionaries Johann Friedrich Gößling and Ernst Homann, and two lay brethren, Hermann Vogelsang and Ernst Jakob. Leaving the Barossa Valley town of Tanunda, they overlanded for 3 months before establishing a mission at Lake Killalpaninna in the Lake Eyre region. The mission, known as Bethesda Mission, was established to convert Dieri (Diyari)-speaking peoples to the Old Lutheran form of Christianity.

A third Old Lutheran mission set off from another Barossa Valley town, Bethany, to establish Hermannsburg on the banks of the Finke River in Central Australia in 1877. Hermannsburg became the most significant of all Lutheran missions to the Aboriginal people of Australia for several reasons. Most importantly, perhaps, has been the longevity and continuity of relations between the Old Lutherans and the Western Aranda people in whose Country the mission was established. Operated by Lutheran missionaries between 1877 and 1982, the establishment of Hermannsburg commenced a relationship between Lutheran Christianity, the Western Aranda and other Aboriginal peoples (Anangu) in Central Australia that continues to endure.[23] Although now headquartered in Alice Springs, the Finke River Mission started at Hermannsburg still operates today. It

Made in Germany 23

continues to deliver Church services to remote Aboriginal communities and to provide welfare support to Indigenous people who adhere to the Lutheran faith.[24] The depth of this relationship is evident in the Lutheran Church in Alice Springs. Here services take place in Aranda and Pitjantjatjara as well as English. Symbols and designs drawn from the Indigenous cultures of Central Australia are evident throughout the building and suggest an organisation that has been engaged in the business of reconciliation for a long time. The recent tour of the Central Australian Women's Choir to Germany underlined the ongoing significance of the relationship, when this group of Aranda, Luritja and Pitjantjatjara women sang Lutheran hymns first introduced to their peoples in the nineteenth century to audiences to whom these songs had been lost.[25]

The enduring relationship between the Indigenous peoples of Australia and the descendants of the Old Lutherans who came to South Australia to escape religious persecution in the 1830s is itself an uncommon thing in settler-colonial Australia, where genuine respectful and committed relationships between settler-colonists and Indigenous peoples are an extreme rarity, and the relationships that do exist are overwhelmingly transactional and fleeting in nature.[26] That the relationship between Lutheran mission, Western Aranda and other Indigenous peoples has endured is remarkable given the fact, as Marcia Langton points out, that most settler Australians only know Aborigines through the stories of former colonists.[27] Where they do exist as interpersonal relationships, they exist for reasons of political expediency and are utilitarian, a means to an end. Relationships of the kind documented by Kim Mahood in her study of cross-cultural engagements in remote Australia are exceedingly rare and highly unusual.[28] To many contemporary Australians, the long association between Old Lutherans and the Western Aranda, Luritja and Pitjanjatjara peoples of Central Australia may seem out of step with current understandings of relations between Indigenous peoples and Christian Church and mission, where Christian interventions are assessed as negative. Instead, the enduring relationship between the Old Lutheranism of the Finke River Mission and Indigenous peoples today suggests that another reading of Church and mission is required that takes into consideration Indigenous understandings and, more importantly, past and present agency.

Universal claims grounded in incorrect understandings of Indigenous people as representatives of a reified culture who stand in opposition to modernity and global world culture are found wanting when applied to the relationship between the Finke River Mission and the Indigenous peoples of Central Australia. Central to our assessment of Lutheran mission at Hermannsburg is a focus on the agency of Western Aranda, Luritja and Pitjantjatjara peoples as active participants in the history of Lutheran mission and the uptake of forms of education and work. We categorically reject the notion of Aboriginal people as passive, and of traditional

24 *Barry Judd*

forms of decision-making as lacking the capability to successfully navigate and negotiate the circumstances of settler-colonialism in which they have found themselves from the 1860s to the present. The history of the Finke River Mission at Hermannsburg should not be seen as a relationship between vastly unequal partners, but as one where the relative power that existed between the partners changed over time, sometimes favouring the missionaries, and sometimes favouring the Indigenous peoples. Jettisoning the common claims of Aboriginal people as incapable, soft and weak, it might be said that the establishment of Hermannsburg on the Finke River in 1877 witnessed the meetings of equals – as the hard laws of Old Lutheranism from Prussia met the hard laws of the Western Aranda. Aranda law men from Central Australia met the Prussian missionaries as their equals. They did so because of a coincidence. The two law systems converged in the foundational symbol of the cross. The missionaries had cut the crucifix into a tree on the Finke River. The Western Aranda men who saw this symbol, one that lay at the heart of their own system of morals, ethics and cosmological understandings of human origins, believed that those who had crafted it must themselves also be men of law.[29] The perceived overlap between Old Lutheranism and Alcheringa (Western Aranda religious beliefs to the Luritja and Pitjantjatjara known as Tjukurrpa) therefore provided the common ground and foundation on which the relationship between the Finke River Mission and Indigenous peoples in Central Australia was built. Later the Western Aranda would find what they regarded to be a footprint of Jesus in the bed of the Finke River, a sign which they used to assimilate and justify the coming together of Christian law with their own religion based in Alcheringa.[30] Jesus had been in their Country since the time of creation and the coming of the Old Lutheran missionaries was necessary to reveal this truth to the Western Aranda and the other peoples of Central Australia. The coincidence of the cross is important not only because it diminished the possibility of a violent response to the incursion of strangers to Western Aranda territories in their initial meeting with the men from Prussia, but also because the perceived commonality it provided enabled an exchange of ideas between the partners. The ideas and insights exchanged back and forth across the cultural divide thus included knowledge and insights of traditional desert societies.

The first missionaries at Hermannsburg included Pastor Hermann Kempe who, upon making contact with the Western Aranda, commenced to create word lists that documented their language.[31] This was a learning that the Old Lutherans believed to be a necessary educative step in their mission to the Aboriginal peoples of Central Australia. An approach to mission work that required Old Lutheran missionaries to learn and become competent in the vernacular language of the peoples with whom they worked was fundamental to their particular brand of

Made in Germany 25

evangelical Christianity.[32] It followed the doctrine of the founder of Protestant Lutheranism Martin Luther, whose breakaway from the Church of Rome sought to ground faith in grass-roots communities with communications between congregations and God direct and through the local tongue rather than through the disconnected route of Latin, a language only understood by a highly educated and elite priesthood. To the Old Lutherans and their mission to the Finke River, the task of understanding the local language and culture was a fundamental task in their work to convert Aboriginal souls to Lutheran Christianity. The importance that Old Lutheran missionaries placed on gaining insight and understanding of the local language, culture and beliefs became a key characteristic of the Finke River Mission to the Aboriginal peoples of Central Australia.

The linguistic work that Pastor Kempe commenced in the 1870s was built upon most famously by Carl Strehlow, who became head missionary at Hermannsburg in 1894 until his death in 1922.[33] A brilliant intellect, Strehlow developed on the earlier linguistic work of his missionary predecessors to successfully document the grammars of Western Aranda and Luritja. In this work, he was helped by his previous linguistic success in documenting the Dieri grammar while a missionary at Bethesda. In addition to his work as a linguist, Carl Strehlow was interested in the ceremonial aspects of Central Australian Aboriginal cultures, becoming a confidant of senior ceremonial leaders known as inkata (law men). Strehlow became a keen ethnographic observer of Indigenous religious practices, and between 1907 and 1920 published in German his monumental work in five volumes *Die Aranda- und Loritja-Stämme in Zentral-Australien* (The Aranda and Luritja Tribes in Central Australia).[34] This work became a success in Germany and elsewhere in continental Europe but was largely ignored in settler-Australia and the global Anglo-sphere. As both missionary and intellectual, Strehlow came to adopt a very pragmatic approach to the relationship between the Lutheranism he had helped import to Central Australia and the ancient religions they sought to replace through the conversion of Aranda and Luritja souls. Yet ultimately his work aimed at displacing the old religions of Australia. Those sceptical of Christian mission might say that the keen intellectual interest Strehlow took in understanding the language and culture of the Western Aranda and Luritja was a means to an end, in that he established himself as an authority on Australian Aboriginal language and culture at least in continental Europe. But his interest in the language and cultural traditions of the Aboriginal peoples of Central Australia was primarily undertaken with the purpose of making the work of the Finke River Mission more effective by developing complex understandings and insights of Aranda and Luritja ontological beliefs and practices.

26 *Barry Judd*

As a missionary and scholar, Carl Strehlow believed that the Aranda and Luritja had to be won over to the side of Old Lutheran Christianity through dialogue, argument and example. At Hermannsburg, Carl Strehlow and his fellow missionaries had to demonstrate that Lutheranism, with its offer of redemption and everlasting life, offered a superior religious option to the old religions based in Country Alcheringa/Tjukurpa. The work of the Finke River Mission was therefore progressed through persuasive discussion and necessarily became philosophical in character. In other words, the linguistic and ethnographic work of Carl Strehlow was necessary to build a framework in which an ongoing cross-cultural dialogue could take place. This approach to Christian mission is often overlooked and downplayed in historical analysis of settler-colonial relations in Australia. The approach Strehlow adopted at Hermannsburg in both his secular academic pursuits and in Christian mission stands in sharp contrast to his rival in the study of Central Australian peoples, University of Melbourne Professor of Biology, Walter Baldwin Spencer.[35] Far better known in Australia than Carl Strehlow, Spencer became the leading expert on 'classical' Aboriginal culture and belief as a result of his research in Central Australia that commenced in 1894 with his membership of the Horn Scientific Expedition. In collaboration with Frank Gillen, postmaster of the Alice Springs Telegraph Station, Spencer documented the religious beliefs and practices of the central Aranda. Their 1899 work *Native Tribes of Central Australia* became highly influential – shaping academic, popular and governmental discourse about Aboriginal people.[36] For example, it was Spencer who mistranslated the Aranda word Alcheringa into English as Dreamtime, a term that became emblematic in the national imagination of Australia as shorthand for Aboriginal culture and spirituality. While Strehlow used his ethnographic insights of Aranda religious practices and beliefs to persuade the Aranda and Luritja to change their beliefs and practices via dialogue as an exchange of ideas, Spencer instead used his work to argue for the settler-colonial state to bring their coercive power to bear on Aboriginal people to force change. In 1911 he became the most senior Australian government official in the Northern Territory as special commissioner and Protector of Aborigines, a position that enabled him to enact his ideas for Aboriginal assimilation including the propagation of the Stolen Generations.

The work of Carl Strehlow is critical to the story of his successor at the Finke River Mission, F. W. Albrecht.[37] Strehlow's untimely death in 1922 precipitated the need for the Finke River Mission to find a replacement for the role of head missionary. When Albrecht arrived to take up his role at Hermannsburg in 1926, he inherited a methodology of work that shaped relations between Old Lutheran missionaries and the western Aranda-Luritja, one characterised by the need for deep cultural insights

Made in Germany 27

and cross-cultural dialogue.[38] The ability to communicate and find common understandings across cultural divides was fundamental to the Old Lutheran mission at Hermannsburg, and Albrecht followed Strehlow in making a personal commitment to have insight into the local culture of the Aboriginal peoples with whom he worked. As we will see in the next chapter, in the era defined by his work and leadership, F. W. Albrecht built on the foundational work of those who preceded him. Unlike Kempe and Strehlow however, Albrecht used his insights and understanding of Aranda language, culture, and religion not only as a pathway to spiritual salvation through the conversation of Aboriginal souls but also as a route to position the western Aranda and Luritja as active economic participants in the regional and national economies of twentieth-century settler-colonial Australia. The chapters that follow therefore speak to the secular work of Albrecht in the spheres of education, training, employment and enterprise as demonstrations of the Enlightenment ideas that shaped his actions and agendas.

Lutheran Reformation: A Precursor to German Enlightenment

Having outlined in brief the coming of the Old Lutherans to Australia and their mission to Aboriginal peoples in South Australia, and before we come to discuss F. W. Albrecht as an individual whose work put into practice Enlightenment ideas, we need to ask what the activity of missionaries in Central Australia has to do with the so-called 'European' Enlightenment that took place in the seventeenth and eighteenth centuries. In our view, the Old Lutherans and the mission they established on the Finke River in Central Australia have much to do with the central ideas embodied in the Enlightenment. These peoples from Prussia brought with them a cultural framework in which notions of work, duty, personal responsibility, self-improvement and Enlightenment through an education based on truth were central. To understand why we make such claims, we need to briefly recall the emergence of Lutheranism in Europe through the Church founded by Martin Luther in protest of what he believed was the corruption of the Church of Rome. The Protestant Reformation commenced by Luther created a revolution that impacted much more than theological belief, as Lutheran ideas about personal responsibility spread beyond matters of religion to shape how the peoples of Europe came to understand the fundamentals of politics and society, including the basis of social contracts between people and institutions including the state.[39]

Although the subject of ongoing academic debate, the rise of Lutheran Protestantism in northern Europe in the sixteenth century is generally viewed as a necessary precursor to the philosophical thinking

28   Barry Judd

that emerged in the eighteenth century and is now referred to as the Age of Enlightenment.[40] While proto-Protestant movements had emerged before Lutheranism and had become more prevalent at the time European society was in transition from the medieval period to that known as the Renaissance, it was the actions of the German and Augustinian friar Martin Luther (1483–1546) that resulted in the Protestant Reformation. Luther, who was also Professor of Moral Theology at the University of Wittenberg and a well-known preacher in the town, was motivated to change and reform owing to the increasing reliance and usage of indulgences by Church and Pope in his native Germany. An indulgence was a theological mechanism used by the medieval Church to grant either partial or full remission from the punishment of sin. The granting of indulgences rested on two important theological beliefs held by Church of Rome. It was thought that penance was insufficient to have the guilt of sin forgiven through absolution alone; one also needed to undergo a temporal form of punishment. Indulgences also rested on a belief in purgatory, a place in the next life where the accumulated debt of an individual sin could be paid off.

In the early sixteenth century, the Church of Rome had committed itself to rebuild St Peter's Basilica on a grand style that demonstrated Christendom's eternal gratitude to God Almighty. In Germany, the Pope approved the sale of special plenary indulgences which gave the buyers of these pieces of paper a remission of the temporal punishment of sin. The man responsible for the sale of the Pope's indulgences in Germany was the Cardinal Archbishop of Mainz, Albrecht von Brandenburg. His sale of indulgences not only provided the funds the Pope needed to build his new Basilica, but also generated new wealth for Albrecht himself. Martin Luther wrote to Albrecht on 31 October 1517 and his letter, the 'Disputation on the Power and Efficacy of Indulgences,' better known as the Ninety-five Theses, commenced the Protestant Reformation.[41] Luther protested that individuals could not buy their way into heaven through the purchases of indulgences. Instead, he claimed that rebirth in the kingdom of heaven was only possible through faith in Jesus alone. Buying one's way into heaven through indulgences (if wealthy) or through good works (if poor) was not possible in his view, as he rejected the notion of purgatory as a place where sin could be absolved. Luther also believed that the Bible alone contained the true word of God. It was a view that made the power and authority of the priesthood secondary, and perhaps even unnecessary. Luther also argued that to end the corruption that characterised the present age, the Church of Rome needed to return to the teachings and practices of the Church at the time of the disciples. He therefore argued for the Church to get back to basics, to an evangelical Church grounded in the vernacular ways of life of the communities of people whose spiritual well-being it sought to shepherd. Luther was

Made in Germany 29

inspired in this thinking by the Ethiopian Church, which has continued to practice faith in ways that mirrored those of the original evangelists.[42] These claims represented a fundamental theological disagreement with Catholic orthodoxy and can be summed up in Luther's claim that human salvation rests on grace alone, faith alone and scripture alone.[43] As we argue later, the core theological understandings of Lutheranism were rearticulated in the Age of Enlightenment to become freedom, individuality, responsibility and culture in ways that would not have been possible within the pre-Reformation Roman Catholic tradition. It is also important to note that Archbishop Albrecht was the younger brother of the Elector of Brandenburg, who was the most powerful of the German Princes at this time. The act of protest by Luther therefore carried with it very serious potential consequences – both religious and political – including the possibility that he be burnt to death at the stake for acts of heresy. His protest needs to be considered a revolutionary act for the forces of change it unleashed and the monopoly on European religion it destroyed.

While many believe that Luther's intention in writing his Ninety-five Theses was to generate scholarly debate within the learned circles of the Catholic Church, his protest led to the political and religious break-up of the Holy Roman Empire within a decade, as the Princes of northern Germany embraced the new Lutheran Church as their Church of state. This process took place through a number of meetings called Diets convened by the Holy Roman Emperor. The schism Luther created in the Catholic Church had several other material consequences, many of which have continued to impact the religious, social and political cultures of Europe and the world since the beginnings of Protestant Lutheranism. Lutheranism succeeded where earlier proto-forms of Protestantism failed, in large part because Luther's protest came after the invention of the printing press.[44] The spread of printing presses allowing his reform agenda to be directly communicated to a mass audience. The printing press and the mass-produced pamphlets, essays and books that were now possible to produce underpinned popular support for the religious reforms set out by Martin Luther. Further, the proliferation of printing presses underpinned Lutheran belief that the Bible is the one and only true source of God's word and that an effective Church is one grounded in the vernacular language and culture of the congregation and community it exists to serve and guide in religious matters.

Once the political implications of his protest became apparent, Luther turned his attention to translating the Bible into German and mapping out the structure of a new Church based on an organisational structure grounded in local congregations and reliant on lay pastors rather than a professional and elite priesthood. Before Luther, the priesthood had acted as the conduit between God and people, with the voice of God and

30 Barry Judd

the teachings of Jesus unintelligible to all but those who belonged to the religious orders and the aristocratic classes who understood the language of the Catholic mass, Latin. After Luther, the people no longer required a priesthood to act as a conduit to God; instead they needed only the ability to read and write in their vernacular language and access to a printed Bible. The theological reforms introduced by Luther contained several characteristics that would become fundamental to further changes that would take place within European politics and society in the centuries that followed, including the Enlightenment of the eighteenth century. Lutheran theology, based on the idea of faith alone as the only way to God's grace, therefore directed responsibility towards the individual and away from a reliance on a professional and hierarchical priesthood and the institution of the Church they embodied.[45] It was an idea centred on the individual and the choices that we ourselves must make. In later centuries, the political philosophers of the Enlightenment would consider freedom and autonomy as the first principles to finding human happiness and the good life.

The notion that the Bible alone was the true source of the word of God and the teachings of Jesus had similarly long-term implications. It required a person to be functionally literate in order to connect with God and find salvation. The Protestant Reformation commenced by Martin Luther therefore provided a major impetus for reading and writing to spread beyond the clerical and aristocratic classes to what would become a growing petit bourgeois or middle class. By centring the Bible as the only true word of God, Lutheranism made education and learning central to the spiritual well-being of the individual.[46] Education in the form of literacy became an essential capability that was necessary in order to find a pathway to heaven. The central role that education played in underpinning Lutheran Protestantism is perhaps hardly surprising. Martin Luther himself was involved in scholarly debates through his role as Professor of Moral Theology. He started the Reformation by writing an academic thesis and in the years that followed he would defend his project and the new Church he founded through a body of writing that would become the basis of a Lutheran intellectual tradition.

Among his most important and influential writings was the *Small Catechism*, an educative tool used to introduce children and others to the fundamentals of Christianity.[47] The catechism contains a Table of Duties that refers to the 10 commandments of God but also references relevant passages of the Bible as a way to instruct and remind members of the three estates of their duties and responsibilities under God. The first section of the Table of Duties addresses members of the ecclesial estate, both preachers and hearers. The second portion addresses members of the civil estate, citizens. And finally, the last portion speaks to the family. Significantly, through this Table Luther placed the concept of duty at the

Made in Germany **31**

centre of his teachings and the Lutheran Church he worked to establish in Germany. The Table of Duties contains a list of biblical extracts that today looks exceedingly conservative and regressive in making patriarchal power the basis of faith. At the time they were written, however, they were considered progressive as they spoke to the fundamental theological differences between Lutherans and Papists, with the former making personal action and responsibility central to faith and salvation. Luther, while not a Papist, was not a true revolutionary and the list of duties he included in the *Small Catechism* was in part written to honour and respect tradition, as all social institutions existed because of God's grace. This fact is clearly seen in his reference to civil society where he quotes several passages that reference duty to worldly authority and the responsibility of subjects or citizens to obey their laws of their Prince or King. For example, Citing Romans 13: 1–4, Luther says of civil government:

> Everyone must submit himself to the governing authorities, for there is no authority except that which God has established. The authorities that exist have been established by God. Consequently, he who rebels against the authority is rebelling against what God has instituted, and those who do so will bring judgment on themselves. For rulers hold no terror for those who do right, but for those who do wrong. Do you want to be free from fear of the one in authority? Then do what is right and he will commend you. For he is God's servant to do you good. But if you do wrong, be afraid, for he does not bear the sword for nothing. He is God's servant, an agent of wrath to bring punishment on the wrong doer.
>
> Rom. 13:1–4

Speaking to subjects or citizens Luther quotes the following passages of the Bible:

> Give to Caesar what is Caesar's, and to God what is God's.
>
> Matt. 22:21

> It is necessary to submit to the authorities, not only because of possible punishment but also because of conscience. This is also why you pay taxes, for the authorities are God's servants, who give their full time to governing. Give everyone what you owe him: If you owe taxes, pay taxes; if revenue, then revenue; if respect, then respect; if honor, then honor.
>
> Rom. 13:5–7

> I urge, then, first of all, that requests, prayers, intercession and thanksgiving be made for everyone—for kings and all those in authority, that

32 *Barry Judd*

we may live peaceful and quiet lives in all godliness and holiness. This is good and pleases God our Savior.

1 Tim. 2:1–3

Remind the people to be subject to rulers and authorities, to be obedient, to be ready to do whatever is good.

Titus 3:1

Submit yourselves for the Lord's sake to every authority instituted among men: whether to the king, as the supreme authority, or to governors, who are sent by him to punish those who do wrong and to commend those who do right.

1 Peter 2:13–14

The centrality of duty and respect for authority in Protestant Lutheranism would also have important consequences for post-Reformation Europe. Combined with a commitment to vernacular culture, the teachings of Martin Luther and the emphasis they placed on the concepts of duty and responsibility in civil matters have been read critically as creating the conditions that allowed the authoritarian regime of Adolf Hitler and the Nazi Party to successfully pervert and corrupt German politics and society in ways that led to immoral acts (contrary to the ten commandments) on a mass scale. Yet, the core commitments of Luther and the Church he established – to a relationship with God that critically relied on literacy and learning – would also establish the conditions for the libertarian ideals and free thinking based on reason of the age known as the European Enlightenment.

Unsurprisingly, many of the key thinkers associated with what became known as the German Enlightenment were Lutherans. Even when their philosophical development came to reject orthodox theological doctrine their conclusions about ethics and morality and what constitutes good and proper human behaviour were influenced by Lutheran teachings. Leading figures of the German Enlightenment who were Lutherans included Immanual Kant, George Wilhelm Frederick Hegel, Johann Gottlieb Fichte and Johann Gottfried von Herder. Kant, for example, was brought up in a Pietist household that stressed religious devotion, humility and a literal interpretation of the Bible.[48] Hegel was educated at Tübinger Stift, a Lutheran seminary attached to the University of Tübingen and Fichte educated under the tutelage of a Lutheran pastor. Herder – who grew up in a poor household – educated himself using his father's Lutheran Bible and Hymn book to learn to read and write.[49] The contribution these thinkers made to the Age of Enlightenment (and also to the Age of Romanticism that developed from it) is so broad in scope and so significant to modern understandings of reality, learning and values that it

Made in Germany **33**

is impossible within the confines of this book to consider how the ideas of each were shaped by their religious upbringings. The connections can, however, be explained with brief reflections and reference to the works of Kant, his student Herder and Hegel, all of whom influenced and argued for and against each other's intellectual projects.

Kant is today remembered as a giant of the German Enlightenment and a key thinker in the development of social contract-based liberalism. Among his most important writings were the 1781 *Critique of Pure Reason* (second edition 1787) and the 1785 *Groundwork of the Metaphysics of Morals.*[50] The *Critique* – arguably the starting point of modern Western philosophy – questions the idea that the universe can be known through reference to pure reason alone. Kant, although known as a rationalist philosopher, set out the limits of pure reason by dividing what is known into two categories of things: phenomena – things that exist and are known only by reference to human sensibilities, and noumena – a category of things that exist only as ends in themselves. Through this strategy, Kant can defend the existence of God or a supreme being which he says is a category of noumena: a thing that exists as an end in itself and that humans can deduce *a priori,* that is, independently of their experiences or knowing that reveals itself *a posteri.* Noumena are rare concepts that can be known through pure reason. In the *Groundwork,* Kant sets out to convince his readers that proper moral behaviour is grounded in reason. According to Kant, moral behaviour results when our rationality moves us from treating our fellow beings as mere means to ends to treating them as ends in themselves. The system of morals that Kant develops rests on what he calls the categorical imperative. Practical reason compels us to act morally in ways that mirror the actions of God or supreme being who is conceptually also driven to act in accordance to the laws of reason. In this sense, Kant, born a Lutheran, replaces the God of grace, faith and scripture that Martin Luther committed himself to, with the God of reasoning. Despite this, the system of morality Kant devises is driven by the concept of duty, as the authority of reason binds humankind to act ethically through a sense of duty. In the Enlightenment philosophy of Immanuel Kant then, a Lutheran commitment to duties and responsibilities remains central to his understanding of metaphysics; even if God is no longer regarded as the omnipresent father who sits in heaven but rather exists as a stripped-down pure concept that exists in the world of human reason in noumenal form. Duty is so important to Kant as a motivational force to drive human morality that in his scheme he regards ethical action that is the result of a sense of duty to be the highest and most perfect form of morality. Many scholars who have studied Kantian ethics since the second half of the twentieth century have noted that although Kant himself came to distance himself from his Lutheran upbringing, the ways he framed and sought to solve key problems of a philosophical nature

34 *Barry Judd*

remained shaped and influenced by Lutheranism in ways he himself had little or no insight into.[51]

If the contribution that Kant made to shaping the Enlightenment ends with a form of God that is conceptualised as universal human reason – a conclusion that emphasises universalism and cosmopolitanism and makes the ideal of perpetual world peace a possibility if we will it to be so – the influence of Lutheran Protestantism on Herder took him in a somewhat opposite direction. Herder, a student of Kant, was both a philosopher of the Enlightenment and a Lutheran pastor for most of his adult life. While the philosophy of Kant referenced the Lutheran commitment to duties and responsibilities, Herder reiterated the foundational belief that understanding must be grounded in the vernacular language and culture of particular peoples. Herder is perhaps best remembered today for his writings on culture and his understanding of cultural differences among the peoples of the world in terms of relativism.[52] He was one of the first to argue that individuals can only be understood in the context of their own cultural and linguistic traditions and values. Like Martin Luther before him, Herder was a strong advocate of vernacular languages and had a deep interest in strengthening the German language. In 1772 Herder published *Treatise on the Origin of Language,* in which he challenged the aristocracy to speak German instead of French, and his work advocating a specifically German aesthetics provided an intellectual framework in support of Goethe and the *Sturm und Drang* movement that developed in literature and music.[53] His interest in linguistics led him to conclude that language shaped, influenced and nuanced the way people thought and the particular ways they understood and interacted with the world. This linguistic work would later be strengthened in the nineteenth century by another Lutheran-born philosopher: Alexander von Humboldt.

Beyond linguistics, Herder also took up the study of vernacular cultures. Perhaps one of his greatest intellectual contributions is the study of the Volk (the people) not as a rabble to be despised but as the life spring of national cultures and therefore of nations.[54] According to Herder, nations and their character were shaped by factors that included climate, foreign relations, education and traditions. He asserted that each nation was a perfect reflection of the people, culture and values that constituted it, and that comparison between the nations is therefore impossible. Herder, like the French philosopher Jean Jacques Rousseau, was one of few thinkers of his age to be highly complementary to the tribal peoples of the New World. He references the 'savage' to argue for relativism against the universal cosmopolitanism that his teacher Kant had pressed for. According to Herder 'each nationality contains its centre of happiness within itself, as a bullet the centre of gravity.' So each society is self-contained as regards its values; one society cannot be 'superior' to another and, by implication, one society cannot through time progress to being a 'better'

Made in Germany 35

one. Herder condemns those who would judge another culture by some alleged universal standard by saying:

> the savage who loves himself, his wife and child with quiet joy and glows with joy at the limited activity of his tribe as for his own life, is in my opinion a more real being than that cultivated shadow who is enraptured with the shadow of the whole species.[55]

As a linguist and student of cultural studies, the great contribution that Herder made to the Enlightenment (and also counter Enlightenment and early Romanticism) is his claim that human beings are always in a state of personal and collective becoming and that our true selves are revealed to us through the vernacular in language and national cultures. Fittingly, Herder is memorialised in statue at the Church of St Peter and Paul in Weimar, Germany. Today the Church is also known as Herderkirche (Herder Church) after Johann Gottfried Herder. His interest in the vernacular as the linguistic and cultural conduit that individuals and collectives utilise to progress towards the realisation of their true self carries with it many echoes of the Lutheran belief that salvation can only be gained through a connection with God that is grounded in scripture made accessible to congregations in the vernacular language (and culture), whether German, English, Aranda or Luritja. The cultural relativism that characterises Herder's work in this sense might be considered evangelical.

The third and final thinker of the Age of Enlightenment whose work might be considered to have been influenced and shaped by Lutheran theology is Hegel. As a key thinker of the Enlightenment, Hegel followed Herder in a consideration of the vernacular and the impact of linguistic and cultural difference and diversity in the world. Hegel came to reject the universality claimed by the Kantian schema of pure and practical reason, in favour of a more linguistically, culturally and, most significantly perhaps, historically informed account of human reason. Often overlooked is the fact that Hegel structured his philosophical work in three parts in a way that is reminiscent of the trinity, a belief that remained core to Lutheran theology. Instead of the trinity of father, son and holy spirit, Hegel structured his project according to the philosophy of logic, nature and spirit.[56] Hegel represents a bridge between the universalism advocated by Kant and the relativism that characterises the works of Herder. Hegel, following Kant, believed that reason was the defining feature of humanity and provided a pathway to substantive human improvement. Whereas Kant viewed reason in its most potent form as a synthetic ahistorical and universal concept, Hegel drew inspiration from Herder and considered reason in a historicised form; a form that spoke to differences in language and national character.

36   Barry Judd

Hegel is perhaps best known for his 1807 work *The Phenomenology of Spirit*, where he proposed that the advance of human reason takes place through dialectic relationships, including his most famous example of the lord and bondsman.[57] His dialectical procedure is grounded in the principle of immanence, by which he means assessing truth claims according to their own internal criteria. Importantly, Hegel believes that reality and human self-consciousness are shaped collectively and through our social relations with other human beings, as well as our relationship with the natural world and the cosmos. Unlike Kant, for Hegel reason exists in the world and is not just confined to human beings. His attempts to understand the operation of human reason are underpinned by the concept of *Geist* (which translates to English as an approximation of spirit *and* mind) and the belief that humanity is driven to realise the best version of ourselves, our *Geist*, through the operations of self-determining freedoms. Through time (history) the operational dialectic relationships, such as that between lord and bondsman, master and slave, settler and native, husband and wife, student and teacher (and so on), operate to bring forth consciousness of self and other. Hegel's schema of historical dialectic is both hard, long fought and somewhat pessimistic, as failure to attain true self-consciousness means humanity continues to live in a state of error where thoughts and actions are directed by false self-consciousness. *Phenomenology* argues that because consciousness always includes self-consciousness, there are no 'given' objects of direct awareness not already mediated by thought. In other words, reality exists thought the relationality of objects and human thought or reason.

Unlike Kant, whose philosophical system of morality grounded in metaphysics replaced God as an omnipresent being of Lutheranism with God as a synthetic conceptualisation of pure *a priori* reason, Hegel sought to mediate the two through the phenomenological process. According to Hegelian thought, God is realised only via its particularisation in the minds of 'his' finite material creatures. In our consciousness of God, human beings serve to realise the self-consciousness of God 'himself.' As a result of this process, God exists as a perfect articulation of human self-consciousness. Hegelism is also referred to as 'Absolute idealism,' owing to his system of moving towards the realisation of true self-consciousness through phenomenological dialectic of historical trial, error and correction. The end point of Hegelism's absolute idealism might be considered a true self-consciousness that creates a comprehensible unity and order of all things. The philosophy of Hegel, like that of Herder, was influenced by the Lutheran engagement with the vernacular as a conduit for learning and a pathway to truth. As his phenomenology of spirit was grounded in a process of historical dialectic, Hegel considered that the discovery of reason through discovery of true self-consciousness was possible. Although he rejected the core Lutheran creed of faith alone and

Made in Germany 37

scripture alone, Hegel accepted Martin Luther's Protestant commitment that congregations would come to know God through a personal and direct relationship with 'him.' As someone who professed to be a sincere Lutheran, Hegel affirmed the fundamental principles of Protestantism in his *Elements of the Philosophy of the Right,* where he notes 'the obstinacy that does honor to mankind, to refuse to recognise in conviction anything not ratified by thought.'[58]

In this chapter, we have surveyed the coming of Old Lutherans to South Australia and their mission among the Aboriginal peoples of this British colony in which they settled. We have also provided a short overview of core Lutheran beliefs and how Lutheranism began as a protest by Dr. Martin Luther against what he viewed as the corruption of the Church of Rome. We have also shown how many of the central figures of what became known as the German Enlightenment were born into the Lutheran Church, and that even those who came to replace Lutheranism with reason were shaped by the theological thoughts, ideas and practices of Martin Luther and the brand of Protestantism he founded. We revisit the origin story of the Lutheran Church and several key thinkers of the Age of Enlightenment in Germany as a way to illustrate some of the important continuities that exist between core ideas and practices inherent to Lutheran Protestantism and those carried forward into 'modernity' by the German philosophers Kant, Herder and Hegel, among others. We have done so to show that Lutheran theology and the practices and values embraced and promoted by Martin Luther and his Church were not contained to the realm of theological debate and organised religion. Instead, by the time of the European Enlightenment, they had come to influence German secular society in ways that shaped popular understandings about the value of education, personal duty and responsibility, nation and national culture as expressed through the language, literature and music of the people (*Volk*).

As nineteenth-century immigrants to Australia, the Old Lutherans who commenced mission to the Aboriginal peoples of Central Australia and South Australia not only carried with them the theological understandings of Martin Luther but also the cultural baggage of the German Enlightenment. We argue that the Enlightenment values and ideas of thinkers such as Kant, Herder and Hegel, just as much as Lutheranism, had currency in German politics and society, including how individuals understood personal identity. In making this claim we are interested not so much in the theological doctrines the Old Lutherans imported to Central Australia from Prussia, but in the material effects consequent on the import of their cultural values and practices, which were shaped by Lutheranism either directly through the sixteenth-century teaching of Martin Luther or indirectly through the Enlightenment ideals of the eighteenth and early nineteenth centuries. Values that emphasised vernacular cultures,

38 Barry Judd

learning and education, personal duty and responsibility (work ethic) all find common ground in Lutheran theology and the German Enlightenment.[59] The work of Pastors Kempe and Strehlow at the Finke River Mission at Ntaria (Hermannsburg) described earlier in this chapter exemplifies these values as indicated by their intellectual engagements with *Arandaic* and Western desert linguistics, cultural beliefs and practices.

In the next chapter, we take this argument further by documenting the work of F. W. Albrecht who arrived at Hermannsburg in 1926 to take up the position of head missionary after the death of his predecessor Carl Strehlow several years earlier. We argue that Albrecht, who was born and grew up in East Prussia and served in the field ambulance corps for the German Empire, held views that were significantly shaped by a cultural perspective deeply influenced not only by his own Lutheran faith but also by the ideas of Kant, Herder, Hegel and others who changed Germany as a result of their unrelenting pursuit of reason during the Age of Enlightenment. Through his Lutheran faith, Albrecht was motivated to good works among the Aranda, Luritja and others that focussed on the secular matters of learning, education, employment and enterprise. We therefore argue that Albrecht's secular work among the Aboriginal peoples of Central Australia was shaped by both his German and Lutheran backgrounds. As a result, F. W. Albrecht was directed in his mission to Aboriginal people not by the racist policies and attitudes that shaped settler Anglo-Australian interactions and responses to the natives, but by the core beliefs of Martin Luther as well as by many of the ideas popularised by the German Enlightenment. Just as in Germany, the central tenets of Lutheran Protestantism spilled out into secular society to shape the ways in which thinkers like Kant, Herder and Hegel understood reason, reality, society, politics, culture and religion, at Hermannsburg the same processes occurred. In our view, the work of Albrecht necessarily modulated between, on the one hand, theological doctrine and his task as evangelist to Aboriginal people and, on the other hand, the secular tasks of securing a sound social and economic future for the same people in a contemporary settler Anglo-Australia hostile to their very existence. It is his work in respect of education and learning and employment and enterprise that we understand to be the clearest example of how Albrecht and other Lutherans who dedicated their lives in mission to Aboriginal people were complicit in the import of Enlightenment ideals to Central Australia.

Notes

1 National Inquiry into the Separation of Aboriginal and Torres Strait Islander Children from Their Families (Australia). Bringing Them Home: Report of the National Inquiry into the Separation of Aboriginal and Torres Strait Islander Children from Their Families (Sydney: Human Rights and Equal Opportunity Commission, 1997), https://humanrights.gov.au/our-work/

Made in Germany 39

bringing-them-home-report-1997, accessed 6 March 2023; Anna Haebich, *Broken Circles: Fragmenting Indigenous Families 1800–2000* (Fremantle: Fremantle Arts Centre Press, 2000); Robert Manne, *In Denial: The Stolen Generations and the Right* (Melbourne: Black Inc., 2001); Peter Read, *A Rape of the Soul so Profound: The Return of the Stolen Generation* (St Leonards: Allen and Unwin, 1999); Kevin Rudd, 'Apology to Australia's Indigenous peoples,' Commonwealth House of Representatives *Parliamentary Debates* (13 February 2008), 167–171.

2 Two exceptions are Katharine Massam, Spanish Benedictine Missionary Women in Australia (Canberra: ANU Press, 2020) and Laura Rademaker, *Found in Translation: Many meanings on a North Australian Mission* (Honolulu: University of Hawai'i Press, 2018).

3 For more on Geoffrey Blainey see Richard Allsop, *Geoffrey Blainey: Writer, Historian, Controversialist* (Clayton: Monash University Publishing, 2020).

4 The written details of this talk, one of the many that Blainey gave during this period, are now lost to time. But Blainey's argument is clear in the memory of Judd, who, as the son of a woman whose life was positively changed by Lutheran missionaries, found it particularly striking.

5 Tim Rowse, 'Indigenous Heterogeneity,' *Australian Historical Studies* 43, No. 3 (2014): 297–310; Miranda Johnson and Tim Rowse, 'Indigenous and Other Australians since 1901: A Conversation between Professor Tim Rowse and Dr Miranda Johnson,' *Aboriginal History* 42 (2018): 125–139. Recent scholarship critiquing structuralist approaches includes: Jane Carey and Ben Silverstein, 'Thinking with and beyond Settler Colonial Studies: New Histories after the Postcolonial,' *Postcolonial Studies* 23, No. 1 (2020): 1–20, https://doi.org/10.1080/13688790.2020.1719569; J. Kēhaulani Kauanui, '"A Structure, Not an Event": Settler Colonialism and Enduring Indigeneity,' Forum: Emergent Critical Analytics for Alternative Humanities, *Lateral* 5, No. 1 (2016): n.p.; Shino Konishi, 'First Nations Scholars, Settler Colonial Studies, and Indigenous History,' *Australian Historical Studies* 50, No. 3 (2019): 285–304, https://doi.org/10.1080/1031461X.2019.1620300.

6 See Richard Hauser, 'Australian Lutheran Schooling: A Historical Perspective,' *Lutheran Theological Journal* 37, No. 3 (2003): 111–118; Everard Leske, *For Faith and Freedom: The Story of Lutherans and Lutheranism in Australia, 1838–1996* (Adelaide: Open Book Publishers, 1996); Maurice E. Schild and Philip J. Hughes, *The Lutherans in Australia* (Canberra: Australian Government Publishing Service, 1996).

7 For an overview of F. W. Albrecht's Life and Interactions with Aboriginal Australians, see Barbara Henson, *A Straight-Out Man: F.W. Albrecht and Central Australian Aborigines* (Parkville: Melbourne University Press, 1992).

8 Daniel Tröhler, 'The Educationalization of the Modern World: Progress, Passion, and the Protestant Promise of Education,' in *Educational Research: The Educationalization of Social Problems, eds. Paul Smeyers and Marc Depaepe (Educational Research. Dordrecht: Springer Netherlands, 2008), 31–46.*

9 Sunkar Muthu, *Empire and Modern Political Thought* (New York: Cambridge University Press, 2012); Sunkar Muthu, *Enlightenment Against Empire* (Princeton, NJ: Princeton University Press, 2003); W. Mignolo, 'Delinking: The Rhetoric of Modernity, the Logic of Coloniality and the Grammar of Decoloniality,' *Cultural Studies* 21, No. 2 (2007): 449–514; A. Quijano, 'Coloniality and Modernity/Rationality,' *Cultural Studies* 21, No. 2 (2007): 168–178.

10 A recent study of British slavery seeks to trace this legacy. See the Legacies of British Slavery project, https://www.ucl.ac.uk/lbs/, accessed 2 December 2022.

11 Mark McKenna, *Return to Uluru* (Melbourne: Black Inc., 2021), 162.

40 *Barry Judd*

12 For a detailed account of the incident and its aftermath, see McKenna, *Return to Uluru.*

13 Rick Lewis, 'Kant 200 Years On,' *Philosophy Now* 49 (February 2005): n.p., https://philosophynow.org/issues/49/Kant_200_Years_On, accessed on 2 December 2022.

14 Andrew Louth, 'Old Prussian Union,' in *The Oxford Dictionary of the Christian Church*, Fourth edition (Oxford University Press, Online Edition, 2022).

15 David Gerber, 'The Pathos of Exile: Old Lutheran Refugees in the United States and South Australia,' *Comparative Studies in Society and History* 26, No. 3 (1984): 498–522.

16 D. Van Abbè, 'Kavel, August Ludwig Christian (1798–1860),' in *Australian Dictionary of Biography*, National Centre of Biography, Australian National University, https://adb.anu.edu.au/biography/kavel-august-ludwig-christian-2287/text2945, published first in hardcopy 1967, accessed online 29 January 2023; David A. Schubert, *Kavel's People: From Prussia to South Australia* (Adelaide: Lutheran Publishing House, 1985).

17 Leske, *For Faith and Freedom;* Charles Myer, '"What a Terrible Thing it is to Entrust One's Children to Such Heathen Teachers": State and Church Relations Illustrated in the Early Lutheran Schools of Victoria,' *History of Education Quarterly* 40, No. 3 (2000): 302–319.

18 'Angas, George Fife (1789–1879), in *Australian Dictionary of Biography*, National Centre of Biography, Australian National University, https://adb.anu.edu.au/biography/angas-george-fife-1707/text1855, published first in hardcopy 1966, accessed online 29 January 2023.

19 Christine Lockwood argues that Fife Angas and the Dresden missionaries were at odds with how they viewed the treatment of Aboriginal people and question of 'civilising' Christianity. Christine Lockwood, '"We hold you to be servants of the Christian church of the Lutheran confession among the heathen": The Missiology of the Dresden Missionaries in Australia,' *Lutheran Theological Journal* 47, No. 2 (2013): 80–90; Christine Lockwood, 'The Two Kingdoms: Lutheran Missionaries and the British Civilising Mission in Early South Australia' (PhD Thesis: University of Adelaide, 2014). See also Anne Scrimgeour, 'Colonizers as Civilizers: Aboriginal Schools and the Mission to "civilise" in South Australia, 1839–1845' (PhD Thesis: Charles Darwin University, 2007).

20 Rob Amery, *Warraparna Kaurna!: Reclaiming an Australian Language* (Adelaide: University of Adelaide Press, 2016).

21 Anne Scrimgeour, 'Notions of Civilisation and the Project to "Civilise" Aborigines in South Australia in the 1840s,' *History of Education Review* 35, No. 1 (2006): 35–46.

22 See Felicity Jensz, '"Poor heathens", "Cone-headed natives" and "Good water": The Production of Knowledge of the Interior of Australia through German Texts From around the 1860s,' *Postcolonial Studies* 21, No. 1 (2018): 100.

23 Peggy Brock and Jacqueline Van Gent, 'Generational Religious Change among the Arrernte at Hermannsburg, Central Australia,' *Australian Historical Studies* 33, No. 120 (2002): 303–318.

24 See the Finke River Mission website on current operations: https://finkerivermission.lca.org.au/, accessed 28 January 2023.

25 Their journey was documented in Naina Sen, *The Song Keepers* (Screen Australia and Brindle Films, 2017).

Made in Germany 41

26 Paul G. E. Albrecht, 'The Finke River Mission Approach to Mission Work among Aborigines in Central Australia,' *Lutheran Theological Journal* 32, No. 1 (1998): 7–15.

27 Marcia Langton, '*Well, I heard it on the radio and I saw it on the television...': an Essay for the Australian Film Commission on the Politics and Aesthetics of Filmmaking by and about Aboriginal People and Things* (North Sydney, NSW: Australian Film Commission, 1993).

28 Kim Mahood, *Craft for a Dry Lake: A Memoir* (Sydney: Anchor, 2000); Kim Mahood, *Wandering with Intent: Essays* (Brunswick: Scribe Publications, 2022).

29 Jonathan Matthews and Pru Colville, *The Dream and the Dreaming: An Unlikely Alliance Between German Missionaries and the Aboriginal People of Central Australia* (ABC TV/CoJo Productions, 2003).

30 Diane Austin-Broos, 'Narratives of the Encounter at Ntaria,' *Oceania* 65, No. 2 (1994): 131–50.

31 Kempe compiled the first Aranda book of Christian instruction and worship. Adolf Hermann Kempe, *Galtjintana-pepa: kristianirberaka mbontala* (Hermannsburg: Missionshandlung, 1891).

32 Heidi Marie Kneebone, 'The Language of the Chosen View: The First Phase of Graphization of Dieri by Hermannsburg Missionaries, Lake Killalpaninna, 1867–80' (PhD Thesis: University of Adelaide, 2005); David Moore, 'The Reformation, Lutheran Tradition and Missionary Linguistics,' *Lutheran Theological Journal* 49, No. 1 (2015): 36–48.

33 Diane Austin-Broos, 'Of Kinship and Other Things: T. G. H. Strehlow in Central Australia,' in *German Ethnography in Australia*, eds. Nicolas Peterson and Anna Kenny (Canberra: ANU Press, 2017), 169–193; Anna Kenny 'Early Ethnographic Work at the Hermannsburg Mission in Central Australia, 1877–1910,' in *German Ethnography in Australia*, eds. Peterson and Kenny, 223–241.

34 Carl Strehlow, *Die Aranda-und Loritja-Stämme in Zentral-Australien* (Frankfurt am Main: Joseph Baer and Co., 1907–1920).

35 Walter F. Veit, 'Strehlow, Carl Friedrich (1871–1922),' in *Australian Dictionary of Biography*, National Centre of Biography, Australian National University, https://adb.anu.edu.au/biography/strehlow-carl-friedrich-8698/text15221, published first in hardcopy 1990, accessed online 29 January 2023.

36 Baldwin Spencer and Francis J. Gillen, *The Native Tribes of Central Australia* (London: Macmillan, 1899).

37 Austin-Broos, 'Of Kinship and Other Things'; Kenny, 'Early Ethnographic Work at the Hermannsburg Mission in Central Australia.'

38 Warwick Anderson, 'Hermannsburg, 1929: Turning Aboriginal "Primitives" into Modern Psychological Subjects,' *Journal of the History of the Behavioral Sciences* 50, No. 2 (2014): 127–147.

39 Wanda Deifelt, 'Advocacy, Political Participation, and Citizenship: Lutheran Contributions to Public Theology,' *Dialog* 49, No. 2 (2010): 108–114.

40 Douglas Clark Baxter, 'The Impact of the Reformation,' *The Historian* 58, No. 2 (1996): 446–448; Albrecht Beutel, 'Martin Luther in the German Enlightenment,' in *Oxford Research Encyclopedia of Religion* online version, 27 March 2017. https://doi.org/10.1093/acrefore/9780199340378.013.299; Arthur Geoffrey Dickens, *The German Nation and Martin Luther* (London: Edward Arnold, 1974).

41 Martin Luther, 1483–1546, '95 Theses against Indulgences (English Text),' *Special Collections Online Exhibits*, https://speccoll.library.arizona.edu/online-exhibits/items/show/1373, accessed January 29, 2023.

42   Barry Judd

42 David Daniels, 'Martin Luther and Ethiopian Christianity: Historical Traces,' *Sightings,* 2 November 2017, https://divinity.uchicago.edu/sightings/articles/martin-luther-and-ethiopian-christianity-historical-traces, accessed 28 February 2023. See also Stanislau Paulau, 'An Ethiopian Orthodox Monk in the Cradle of the Reformation: Abba Mika'el, Martin Luther, and the Unity of the Church,' in *Ethiopian Orthodox Christianity in a Global Context: Entanglements and Disconnections,* eds. Stanislau Paulau and Martin Tamcke (Leiden; Boston, MA: Brill, 2022), 81–109.

43 H. J. Hillerbrand, 'Martin Luther,' in *Encyclopedia Britannica,* 4 January 2023, https://www.britannica.com/biography/Martin-Luther, accessed 29 January 2023.

44 Mark U. Edwards Jr., *Printing, Propaganda and Martin Luther* (Berkeley: University of California Press, 1994).

45 Hillerbrand, 'Martin Luther,' n.p.

46 Franklin V. N. Painter, *Luther on Education, Including a Historical Introduction and a Translation of the Reformer's Two Most Important Educational Treatises* (Philadelphia, PA: Lutheran Publication Society, 1889).

47 Martin Luther, *Luther's Small Catechism and Scripture Texts for Schools* (North Adelaide: Lutheran Book Depot, 1940).

48 Manfred Kuehn, *Kant: A Biography* (Cambridge: Cambridge University Press, 2001).

49 Paul Redding, 'Georg Wilhelm Friedrich Hegel,' in *The Stanford Encyclopedia of Philosophy,* ed. Edward N. Zalta (Winter 2020, online edition) https://plato.stanford.edu/archives/win2020/entries/hegel/, accessed 27 January 2023; Dan Breazeale, 'Johann Gottlieb Fichte,' in *The Stanford Encyclopedia of Philosophy,* ed. Edward N. Zalta (Spring 2022 online edition), https://plato.stanford.edu/archives/spr2022/entries/johann-fichte/, accessed 27 January 2023; Michael Forster, 'Johann Gottfried von Herder,' in *The Stanford Encyclopedia of Philosophy,* ed. Edward N. Zalta (Summer 2022 online edition), https://plato.stanford.edu/archives/sum2022/entries/herder/, accessed 27 January 2023. On Herder and colonialism, see V. Spencer, 'Kant and Herder on Colonialism, Indigenous Peoples, and Minority Nations,' *International Theory* 7, No. 2 (2015): 360–392; Joanna Raisbeck, 'Race and Colonialism around 1800: Herder, Fischer, Kleist,' *Publications of the English Goethe Society* 91, No. 2 (2022): 140–156.

50 Immanuel Kant, *Critique of Pure Reason,* trans. J. M. D. Meiklejohn (London: Bohn, 1855); Immanuel Kant, *The Moral Law: Kant's Groundwork of the Metaphysics of Morals,* trans. H. J. Paten (London: Hutchinson, 1951).

51 See Bernard M. G. Reardon, *Kant as Philosophical Theologian* (London: Palgrave Macmillan, 1988); Svend Andersen, 'Kant, Kissinger, and Other Lutherans: On Ethics and International Relations,' *Studies in Christian Ethics* 20, No. 1 (2007): 13–29; Jonathan Head, 'Scripture and Moral Examples in Pietism and Kant's Religion,' *Irish Theological Quarterly* 83, No. 3 (2018): 217–234; Patrick R. Frierson, 'Providence and Divine Mercy in Kant's Ethical Cosmopolitanism,' *Faith and Philosophy* 24, No. 2 (2007): 144–164.

52 Sonia Sikka, *Herder on Humanity and Cultural Difference: Enlightened Relativism* (Cambridge: Cambridge University Press, 2012).

53 Johann Gottfried Herder, 'Treatise on the Origin of Language' (1772), in *J. G. Herder: Philosophical Writings,* trans. and ed. Michael Forster (Cambridge: Cambridge University Press, 2002), 65–164. On the Enlightenment and the Sturm und Drang movement, see James Hardin and Christoph Schweitzer, eds. *German Writers from the Enlightenment to Sturm und Drang, 1720–1764* (Detroit: Gale Research, 1990).

54 For example, his collections of Folk Songs first published in 1778. See Johann Gottfried Herder, *Song Loves the Masses: Herder on Music and Nationalism,* trans. Philip Bohlman (Berkeley: University of California Press, 2016).

Made in Germany 43

55 Quoted in Brian King, 'Herder and Human Identity,' *Philosophy Now* 112 (2016): n.p., https://philosophynow.org/issues/112/Herder_and_Human_Identity, accessed 27 January 2023.
56 Redding, 'Georg Wilhelm Friedrich Hegel.'
57 Georg Wilhelm Friedrich Hegel, *The Phenomenology of Spirit* [1807], trans. Terry Pinkard (Cambridge: Cambridge University Press, 2018).
58 Georg Wilhelm Friedrich Hegel, *Elements of the Philosophy of Right.* Ed. Allen Wood, Trans. H. B Nisbet (Cambridge: Cambridge University Press, 1991).
59 David Moore, 'The Reformation, Lutheran Tradition, and Missionary Linguistics,' in 'German Lutheran Missionaries and the Linguistic Description of Central Australian Languages, 1890–1910' (PhD Thesis: University of Western Australia, 2019), 21–38.

Bibliography

Primary

Hegel, Georg Wilhelm Friedrich. *Elements of the Philosophy of Right.* Edited by Allen Wood, Translated by H. B. Nisbet. Cambridge; New York: Cambridge University Press, 1991.

Hegel, Georg Wilhelm Friedrich. *The Phenomenology of Spirit* [1807]. Translated by Terry Pinkard. Cambridge: Cambridge University Press, 2018.

Herder, Johann Gottfried. *Song Loves the Masses: Herder on Music and Nationalism.* Translated by Philip Bohlman. Berkeley: University of California Press, 2016.

Herder, Johann Gottfried. 'Treatise on the Origin of Language [1772].' In *J. G. Herder: Philosophical Writings*, translated and edited by Michael Forster. Cambridge: Cambridge University Press, 2002.

Kant, Immanuel. *Critique of Pure Reason.* Translated by J. M. D. Meiklejohn. London: Bohn, 1855.

Kant, Immanuel. *The Moral Law: Kant's Groundwork of the Metaphysics of Morals.* Translated by H. J. Paten. London: Hutchinson, 1951.

Kempe, Adolf Hermann. *Galtjintana-pepa: kristianirberaka mbontala.* Hermannsburg: Missionshandlung, 1891.

Luther, Martin. '95 Theses against Indulgences (English text).' In *Special Collections Online Exhibits*, https://speccoll.library.arizona.edu/online-exhibits/items/show/1373, accessed 29 January 2023.

Luther, Martin. *Luther's Small Catechism and Scripture Texts for Schools.* North Adelaide: Lutheran Book Depot, 1940.

Rudd, Kevin. 'Apology to Australia's Indigenous peoples.' Commonwealth House of Representatives *Parliamentary Debates*, 13 February 2008.

Strehlow, Carl. *Die Aranda-und Loritja-Stämme in Zentral-Australien.* Frankfurt am Main: Joseph Baer and Co., 1907–1920.

Secondary

Albrecht, Paul G. E. 'The Finke River Mission Approach to Mission Work among Aborigines in Central Australia.' *Lutheran Theological Journal* 32, Number 1 (1998): 7–15.

Allsop, Richard. *Geoffrey Blainey: Writer, Historian, Controversialist.* Clayton: Monash University Publishing, 2020.

44 *Barry Judd*

Amery, Rob. *Warraparna Kaurna!: Reclaiming an Australian Language.* Adelaide: University of Adelaide Press, 2016.

Andersen, Svend. 'Kant, Kissinger, and Other Lutherans: On Ethics and International Relations.' *Studies in Christian Ethics* 20, Number 1 (2007): 13–29.

Anderson, Warwick. 'Hermannsburg, 1929: Turning Aboriginal "Primitives" into Modern Psychological Subjects.' *Journal of the History of the Behavioral Sciences* 50, Number 2 (2014): 127–147.

'Angas, George Fife (1789–1879).' In *Australian Dictionary of Biography*, National Centre of Biography, Australian National University, https://adb.anu.edu.au/biography/angas-george-fife-1707/text1855, published first in hardcopy 1966, accessed online 29 January 2023.

Austin-Broos, Diane. 'Narratives of the Encounter at Ntaria.' *Oceania* 65, Number 2 (1994): 131–50.

Austin-Broos, Diane. 'Of Kinship and Other Things: T. G. H Strehlow in Central Australia.' In *German Ethnography in Australia*, edited by Nicolas Peterson and Anna Kenny. Canberra: ANU Press, 2017.

Baxter, Douglas Clark. 'The Impact of the Reformation.' *The Historian* 58, Number 2 (1996): 446–448.

Beutel, Albrecht. 'Martin Luther in the German Enlightenment.' In *Oxford Research Encyclopedia of Religion* (online edition, 27 March 2017). https://doi.org/10.1093/acrefore/9780199340378.013.299.

Breazeale, Dan. 'Johann Gottlieb Fichte.' In *The Stanford Encyclopedia of Philosophy*, edited by Edward N. Zalta. Spring 2022 online edition, https://plato.stanford.edu/archives/spr2022/entries/johann-fichte/, accessed 27 January 2023.

Brock, Peggy and Jacqueline Van Gent. 'Generational Religious Change among the Arrernte at Hermannsburg, Central Australia.' *Australian Historical Studies* 33, Number 120 (2002): 303–318.

Carey, Jane and Ben Silverstein. 'Thinking with and beyond Settler Colonial Studies: New Histories after the Postcolonial.' *Postcolonial Studies* 23, Number 1 (2020): 1–20. https://doi.org/10.1080/13688790.2020.1719569.

Daniels, David. 'Martin Luther and Ethiopian Christianity: Historical Traces.' *Sightings*, 2 November 2017, https://divinity.uchicago.edu/sightings/articles/martin-luther-and-ethiopian-christianity-historical-traces, accessed 28 February 2023

Deifelt, Wanda. 'Advocacy, Political Participation, and Citizenship: Lutheran Contributions to Public Theology.' *Dialog* 49, Number 2 (2010): 108–114.

Dickens, Arthur Geoffrey. *The German Nation and Martin Luther.* London: Edward Arnold, 1974.

Edwards Jr., Mark U. *Printing, Propaganda and Martin Luther.* Berkeley: University of California Press, 1994.

Finke River Mission. https://finkerivermission.lca.org.au/, accessed 28 January 2023.

Forster, Michael. 'Johann Gottfried von Herder.' In *The Stanford Encyclopedia of Philosophy* edited by Edward N. Zalta. Summer 2022 online edition, https://plato.stanford.edu/archives/sum2022/entries/herder/, accessed 27 January 2023.

Frierson, Patrick R. 'Providence and Divine Mercy in Kant's Ethical Cosmopolitanism.' *Faith and Philosophy* 24, Number 2 (2007): 144–164.

Made in Germany   45

Gerber, David. 'The Pathos of Exile: Old Lutheran refugees in the United States and South Australia.' *Comparative Studies in Society and History* 26, Number 3 (1984): 498–522.

Haebich, Anna. *Broken Circles: Fragmenting Indigenous Families 1800–2000.* Fremantle: Fremantle Arts Centre Press, 2000.

Hardin, James and Christoph Schweitzer, editors. *German Writers from the Enlightenment to Sturm und Drang, 1720–1764.* Detroit: Gale Research, 1990.

Hauser, Richard. 'Australian Lutheran Schooling: A Historical Perspective.' *Lutheran Theological Journal* 37, Number 3 (2003): 111–118.

Head, Jonathan. 'Scripture and Moral Examples in Pietism and Kant's Religion.' *Irish Theological Quarterly* 83, Number 3 (2018): 217–234.

Henson, Barbara. *A Straight-Out Man: F.W. Albrecht and Central Australian Aborigines.* Parkville, Vic.: Melbourne University Press, 1992.

Hillerbrand, Hans J. 'Martin Luther.' In *Encyclopedia Britannica*, 4 January 2023. https://www.britannica.com/biography/Martin-Luther, accessed 29 January 2023.

Jensz, Felicity. '"Poor heathens", "Cone-headed natives" and "Good water": The Production of Knowledge of the interior of Australia through German Texts from around the 1860s.' *Postcolonial Studies* 21, Number 1 (2018): 96–112.

Johnson, Miranda and Tim Rowse. 'Indigenous and Other Australians since 1901: A Conversation between Professor Tim Rowse and Dr Miranda Johnson.' *Aboriginal History* 42 (2018): 125–139.

Kēhaulani Kauanui, J. '"A Structure, Not an Event": Settler Colonialism and Enduring Indigeneity.' Forum: Emergent Critical Analytics for Alternative Humanities, *Lateral* 5, Number 1 (2016): n.p.

Kenny, Anna. 'Early Ethnographic Work at the Hermannsburg Mission in Central Australia, 1877–1910.' In *German Ethnography in Australia*, edited by Nicolas Peterson and Anna Kenny. Canberra: ANU Press, 2017.

King, Brian. 'Herder and Human Identity.' *Philosophy Now* 112 (2016): n.p., https://philosophynow.org/issues/112/Herder_and_Human_Identity, accessed 27 January 2023.

Kneebone, Heidi Marie. 'The Language of the Chosen View: The First Phase of Graphization of Dieri by Hermannsburg Missionaries, Lake Killalpaninna, 1867–80.' PhD Thesis: Adelaide University, 2005.

Konishi, Shino. 'First Nations Scholars, Settler Colonial Studies, and Indigenous History.' *Australian Historical Studies* 50, Number 3 (2019): 285–304. https://doi.org/10.1080/1031461X.2019.1620300.

Kuehn, Manfred. *Kant: A Biography.* Cambridge: Cambridge University Press, 2001.

Langton, Marcia. *'Well, I heard it on the radio and I saw it on the television...': An Essay for the Australian Film Commission on the Politics and Aesthetics of Filmmaking by and about Aboriginal People and Things.* North Sydney, NSW: Australian Film Commission, 1993.

Legacies of British Slavery Project, https://www.ucl.ac.uk/lbs/, accessed 2 December 2022.

Leske, Everard. *For Faith and Freedom: The Story of Lutherans and Lutheranism in Australia, 1838–1996.* Adelaide: Open Book Publishers, 1996.

Lewis, Rick. 'Kant 200 Years On.' *Philosophy Now* 49 (February 2005): n.p., https://philosophynow.org/issues/49/Kant_200_Years_On, accessed on 2 December 2022.

46 Barry Judd

Lockwood, Christine. 'The Two Kingdoms: Lutheran Missionaries and the British Civilising Mission in Early South Australia.' PhD Thesis: University of Adelaide, 2014.

Lockwood, Christine. '"We hold you to be servants of the Christian Church of the Lutheran confession among the Heathen": The Missiology of the Dresden Missionaries in Australia.' *Lutheran Theological Journal* 47, Number 2 (2013): 80–90.

Louth, Andrew. 'Old Prussian Union.' In *The Oxford Dictionary of the Christian Church*. Fourth edition. Oxford University Press, online edition, 2022.

Mahood, Kim. *Craft for a Dry Lake: A Memoir.* Sydney: Anchor, 2000.

Mahood, Kim. *Wandering with Intent: Essays.* Brunswick: Scribe Publications, 2022.

Manne, Robert. *In Denial: The Stolen Generations and the Right.* Melbourne: Black Inc., 2001.

Matthews, Jonathan and Pru Colville, Dirs. *The Dream and the Dreaming: An Unlikely Alliance between German Missionaries and the Aboriginal People of Central Australia.* ABC TV/CoJo Productions, 2003.

Massam, Katherine. Spanish Benedictine Missionary Women in Australia. Canberra: ANU Press, 2020.

McKenna, Mark. *Return to Uluru.* Melbourne: Black Inc., 2021.

Mignolo, Walter D. 'Delinking: The Rhetoric of Modernity, the Logic of Coloniality and the Grammar of De-coloniality.' *Cultural Studies* 21, Number 2 (2007): 449–514.

Moore, David. 'The Reformation, Lutheran Tradition, and Missionary Linguistics.' In 'German Lutheran Missionaries and the linguistic description of Central Australian languages, 1890–1910.' PhD Thesis: University of Western Australia, 2019.

Moore, David. 'The Reformation, Lutheran Tradition and Missionary Linguistics.' *Lutheran Theological Journal* 49, Number 1 (2015): 36–48.

Muthu, Sankar. *Empire and Modern Political Thought.* New York: Cambridge University Press, 2012.

Muthu, Sunkar. *Enlightenment against Empire.* Princeton, NJ: Princeton University Press, 2003.

Myer, Charles. '"What a Terrible Thing it is to Entrust One's Children to Such Heathen Teachers": State and Church relations Illustrated in the Early Lutheran Schools of Victoria.' *History of Education Quarterly* 40, Number 3 (2000): 302–319.

National Inquiry into the Separation of Aboriginal and Torres Strait Islander Children from Their Families (Australia). Bringing Them Home: Report of the National Inquiry into the Separation of Aboriginal and Torres Strait Islander Children from Their Families. Sydney: Human Rights and Equal Opportunity Commission, 1997. https://humanrights.gov.au/our-work/bringing-them-home-report-1997, accessed 6 March 2023.

Painter, Franklin V. N. *Luther on Education, Including a Historical Introduction and a Translation of the Reformer's Two Most Important Educational Treatises.* Philadelphia, PA: Lutheran Publication Society, 1889.

Paulau, Stanislau. 'An Ethiopian Orthodox Monk in the Cradle of the Reformation: Abba Mika'el, Martin Luther, and the Unity of the Church.' In *Ethiopian*

Made in Germany 47

Orthodox Christianity in a Global Context: Entanglements and Disconnections, edited by Stanislau Paulau and Martin Tamcke. Leiden; Boston, MA: Brill, 2022.

Quijano, Anibal. 'Coloniality and Modernity/Rationality.' *Cultural Studies* 21, Number 2 (2007): 168–178.

Rademaker, Laura. *Found in Translation: Many meanings on a North Australian Mission*. Honolulu: University of Hawai'i Press, 2018.

Raisbeck, Joanna. 'Race and Colonialism around 1800: Herder, Fischer, Kleist.' *Publications of the English Goethe Society* 91, Number 2 (2022): 140–156.

Read, Peter. *A Rape of the Soul So Profound: The Return of the Stolen Generation*. St Leonards: Allen and Unwin, 1999.

Reardon, Bernard M. G. *Kant as Philosophical Theologian*. London: Palgrave Macmillan, 1988.

Redding, Paul. 'Georg Wilhelm Friedrich Hegel.' In *The Stanford Encyclopedia of Philosophy*, edited by Edward N. Zalta. Winter 2020, online edition, https://plato.stanford.edu/archives/win2020/entries/hegel/, accessed 27 January 2023.

Rowse, Tim. 'Indigenous Heterogeneity.' *Australian Historical Studies* 43, Number 3 (2014): 297–310.

Schild, Maurice E. and Philip J. Hughes. *The Lutherans in Australia*. Canberra: Australian Government Publishing Service, 1996.

Schubert, David A. *Kavel's People: From Prussia to South Australia*. Adelaide: Lutheran Publishing House, 1985.

Scrimgeour, Anne. 'Colonizers as Civilizers: Aboriginal Schools and the Mission to 'civilise' in South Australia, 1839–1845.' PhD Thesis: Charles Darwin University, 2007.

Scrimgeour, Anne. 'Notions of Civilisation and the Project to "Civilise" Aborigines in South Australia in the 1840s.' *History of Education Review* 35, Number 1 (2006): 35–46.

Sen, Naina, Dir. *The Song Keepers*. Screen Australia and Brindle Films, 2017.

Sikka, Sonia. *Herder on Humanity and Cultural Difference: Enlightened Relativism*. Cambridge: Cambridge University Press, 2012.

Spencer, Baldwin and F. J. Gillen. *The Native Tribes of Central Australia*. London: Macmillan, 1899.

Spencer, Vicki A. 'Kant and Herder on Colonialism, Indigenous Peoples, and Minority Nations.' *International Theory* 7, Number 2 (2015): 360–392.

Tröhler, Daniel. 'The Educationalization of the Modern World: Progress, Passion, and the Protestant Promise of Education.' In *Educational Research: The Educationalization of Social Problems*, edited by Paul Smeyers and Marc Depaepe. Educational Research. Dordrecht: Springer Netherlands, 2008.

Van Abbè, D. 'Kavel, August Ludwig Christian (1798–1860).' In *Australian Dictionary of Biography*, National Centre of Biography, Australian National University, https://adb.anu.edu.au/biography/kavel-august-ludwig-christian-2287/text2945, published first in hardcopy 1967, accessed online 29 January 2023.

Veit, Walter F. 'Strehlow, Carl Friedrich (1871–1922).' In *Australian Dictionary of Biography*, National Centre of Biography, Australian National University, https://adb.anu.edu.au/biography/strehlow-carl-friedrich-8698/text15221, published first in hardcopy 1990, accessed online 29 January 2023.

2 Albrecht, Hermannsburg and the 'Problem of Work'

Barry Judd

Friedrich Wilhelm Albrecht (1894–1984) should be a well-known and celebrated figure in Australian history. His work among the Aboriginal peoples of Central Australia commenced with his arrival at Hermannsburg in 1926 and ended with his retirement to Adelaide in 1962. In 1958 Australia awarded him an MBE in recognition of his work as superintendent of the Finke River Mission.[1] Albrecht was a deserving recipient of this honour, noted for his tremendous ability to work hard and undergo severe hardship. Unlike many individuals who receive national honours for their work in support of Aboriginal people today, Albrecht was universally respected, and especially so by the Aranda, Luritja and Pitjantjatjara peoples with whom he worked. Today Albrecht continues to be remembered by Aboriginal peoples across Central Australia as a man of high esteem. He is known to Aboriginal peoples as *Ingkarta*, an Aranda word that means both a highly respected and trusted leader, and a man with deep knowledge of spiritual matters.[2]

Although he would become a significant leader within Lutheran Australia, F. W. Albrecht was not of the Old Lutheran community of South Australia. Like other leaders who oversaw the work of the Finke River Mission, he was an import from German Europe. Albrecht was born at Plawanice in Russian Poland to German-speaking parents – Ferdinand Albrecht, a farmer from Kroczyn, and his wife Helene, née Reichwald.[3] During his formative years of education, Albrecht was schooled in the Russian language at a village school. A fall down cellar stairs as a child left him with the permanent injury of being lame in one leg. Setting his sights on a career as a missionary, Albrecht entered the Lutheran mission institute at Hermannsburg, near Hanover, Germany, in 1913. When World War I interrupted his religious studies and missionary aspirations, he joined the German army and, because of his physical disability, was deployed to serve in the medical corps on the Eastern Front.[4] During his war service, Albrecht was awarded the Iron Cross (Second Class) for tending wounded soldiers while under enemy fire. Following the

DOI: 10.4324/9781003281634-3

The 'Problem of Work' 49

Armistice of November 1918, he returned to Hermannsburg, Germany. He completed his course in 1924 and was shortly thereafter invited to work with the Finke River Mission, at Hermannsburg in the Northern Territory. Prior to making the long journey to Central Australia, Albrecht attended a Lutheran seminary in the United States of America for five months in 1925 to improve his English. While in North America he married Minna Gevers at Winnipeg, Canada. The couple arrived in Australia on 18 October 1925. On 14 February 1926, Albrecht was ordained as a pastor in the United Evangelical Lutheran Church of Australia (UELCA) on 14 February 1926 at Nuriootpa, South Australia. He reached Hermannsburg in April of the same year to replace Carl Strehlow as Superintendent of the Finke River Mission.[5] He was naturalised as an Australian citizen in 1931. Towards the end of his life, he would receive a second honour from Germany when the government of the Federal Republic of Germany (West Germany) awarded him the Officer's Cross of the Order of Merit in 1973.[6]

The ability to cope with hard work and hardship, the result of his upbringing as the eldest son of a farmer and the physical and mental trials of warfare, were character attributes that served Albrecht well in his mission work among the Aboriginal peoples of Central Australia.[7] The fact that he was born in Europe during a period of German industrialisation that coincided with a rise in both nationalist sentiment and Prussian militarism is, we think, important when considering the linkages between Lutheran missions in twentieth-century Australia and the central ideas of the Age of Enlightenment that gained currency and influence in the eighteenth century. It is significant that Albrecht became both participant and witness to the end of old Europe. He saw up close the collapse of the imperial royal houses of Germany, Russia and Austro-Hungry and the replacement of the ancient aristocratic social orders by distinctly modern forms of government. These were forms of government, whether liberal or socialist in type, that reflected many of the ideals that emerged from the German Enlightenment and were advocated by thinkers such as Kant, Herder and Hegel. Whether Albrecht had personal insight and recognition of the influence that Enlightenment ideas exerted on his own understanding of the world and subjectivity is unknown, but it is our assertion that such ideas are implicit in the work he undertook as Superintendent at Hermannsburg in Central Australia.

Although it is beyond both the scope and purpose of this book and our capabilities as scholars to engage in theological debates as these relate to Albrecht, his relationship to God and stance on Lutheran doctrine, we can note that he apparently came to adopt a very ambivalent position in respect of the place of Aranda (and other Aboriginal) religion at Lutheran Hermannsburg.[8] Photographs taken during the Albrecht era at

50   *Barry Judd*

Hermannsburg often show images of Aranda, Luritja and Pitjantjatjara men dressed in ceremonial regalia and body paints, including some undertaking ceremonial dance. We also know he engaged in the global trade for Aboriginal cultural objects, including men's ceremonial objects called *Tjuringa* (Law Stones).[9] Such evidence suggests that even if Albrecht was unable to ever reconcile his own Lutheran belief in Jesus and the Christian God with the Aboriginal belief in *alcheringa/tjukurpa* (creative Dreaming) he encountered in Central Australia, he resigned himself to the fact that Christian converts to the Finke River Mission would quietly retain their own religious beliefs and practices while at the same time professing to be committed and good Lutherans themselves.

One way to understand this theological accommodation, which is rare in the history of Christian missions in Australia, is that Albrecht's German upbringing, attitudes and values made him open to the ideas of *Volk* – national character and cultural relativism that the philosophical project of Herder had popularised in Germany.[10] As discussed in the previous chapter, these ideas had found common ground in Lutheranism, with its fundamental commitment to evangelising the teachings of Jesus through the vernacular languages and cultures of Church congregations whether in Germany, the Aranda lands of Central Australia or elsewhere.[11] Albrecht, it should be noted, carried on the work of his predecessors Hermann Kempe and Carl Strehlow in becoming fluent in Aranda as a way to gain insight and understanding of the Aboriginal cultures of Central Australia and to better engage with the people he was tasked with converting to the Lutheran brand of Protestant Christianity.[12] Albrecht's interest and engagement with Aboriginal language and cultures, and understanding of the *Volk* with whom he engaged, made him a type of missionary very different from most of his counterparts from Anglo-Australian backgrounds.

While Albrecht perhaps only begrudgingly came to live with relativism in respect of Arandaic religious beliefs and practices, his embrace of cultural relativism in secular matters is beyond doubt. This commitment is clearly evidenced through his work towards securing material improvements to Aboriginal well-being through the series of training, education and employment schemes that he devised and implemented over the course of his working life.[13] Arguably, his belief and commitment to a working knowledge of the vernacular linguistics and cultures of the Aranda, Luritja and Pitjantjatjara, and the relativist approach he came to adopt, are the foundational determinants of the lifelong relationship he successfully forged with Aboriginal peoples in Central Australia. It is our contention that his Lutheranism *and* his Germanic upbringing and immersion in German culture, values and perspectives are critical to understanding the approach he adopted towards Aboriginal peoples through his mission work. His Germanic upbringing and cultural identity are likewise critical to understanding why his approach and attitude

The 'Problem of Work' 51

towards Aboriginal peoples appear so different from, and indeed often very out of step with, the positions and attitudes adopted by the missions of other Christian Churches, as well as the legislative and policy frameworks of Australian governments during the period 1926–1952 when he was superintendent at Hermannsburg.

Albrecht: Securing an Aboriginal Future

We start this chapter by referencing Albrecht and how his mission to the Aboriginal peoples of Central Australia was shaped by a Lutheran commitment to the vernacular, and the very German idea that the culture, traditions and values of specific peoples matter, drawn from Enlightenment thinkers Herder (cultural relativism) and Hegel (progress through dialectic historicism). We do so because these ideas stand in very stark contrast to the truth about Aboriginal people as it was understood by Anglo-Australia during the twentieth century. Albrecht was directed in his work by a fundamental commitment to the idea that Aboriginal well-being in a future Australia must be grounded in their own (self) recognition and admiration for the Aboriginal past. This idea, one we think he inherited and co-opted from the German Enlightenment, is significant because it required a belief in the inherent value of the cultural traditions and practices that had shaped the Aboriginal past. In addition, Albrecht believed that Aboriginal people needed to reassert pride in their personal and collective identities as the first peoples of Australia, something he believed should be a source of great pride and not one of great shame and embarrassment. He believed that Aboriginal self-awareness of the cultural values and practices that emerged from the Aboriginal past was critical to Aboriginal futures. According to Albrecht, knowledge of the Aboriginal past – and the cultural and linguistic insights this delivered – formed an essential foundation from which individuals and collectives secure in their own identities and the cultural heritage that shaped them could move successfully forward into an Aboriginal future.

In twentieth-century settler-colonial Australia, such ideas were contrary to the common-sense truths that shaped race relations between Aboriginal people and Anglo-Australians. As mentioned previously, Australian settler-colonialism is based on the economics of pastoralism, a zero-sum logic whereby colonial sheep and cattle operations cannot co-exist with Aboriginal peoples on the same territory or Country at the same time.[14] Functioning according to this logic, Australian settler-colonialism was driven to eliminate Aboriginal people either physically through killing in warfare, by murder or rape, or culturally through governments legislating and regulating policy agendas of containment, assimilation, integration and reconciliation. Until the 1970s, most settler-colonial Australians continued to believe in the dying race theory

52 *Barry Judd*

as a common-sense proposition.[15] Dying race theory was an idea that emerged from Social Darwinism and that suggested Aboriginal people were biologically inferior to Anglo-settlers and would 'naturally' die out as a result of competition with the 'white man.' Even the most progressive elements of Anglo-Australian settler-colonial society believed that even if the Aborigines survived as a distinctive 'race,' there would be no place for Aboriginal religion, culture and practices in a 'modern' Australian nation-state.[16] Yet Albrecht, working in the 1930s to the 1960s, foresaw an Australian future in which Aboriginal peoples and their cultural values and traditions would play an active part. He foresaw their continuation as a distinctive part of a 'modern' Australia, where they would be active participants in the national and the global economy through agriculture, the arts, health and education. Biased as he was towards Lutheranism, Albrecht also foresaw a future Australia in which an Aboriginal Church would emerge from the Finke River Mission to become a focus for spiritual and worldly well-being.[17]

Albrecht's conviction that productive and meaningful Aboriginal futures would be grounded in a persistent Aboriginal cultural tradition and pride in being of Aboriginal heritage were ideas whose genealogy may be traced back not only to writings of Luther but also to those of Herder and Hegel. These ideas continue to be 'radical' and 'revolutionary' when considered in the context of Anglo-Australian settler-colonial truths about the Aborigines and their lack of any future in a 'modern' Australian nation-state. Just how revolutionary Albrecht was in his unwavering advocacy and commitment to an Aboriginal future becomes obvious when referenced against the idea that Aboriginal people should have the same rights of citizenship as settler-colonial peoples (the 1967 referendum on Aborigines) and that they should be free to choose how they live their own lives in 'modern' Australia (the 1972 policy of Aboriginal self-determination). The fact that these so-called innovations in settler-colonial Anglo-Australian politics occurred decades after Albrecht committed to Aboriginal futures is a sad indictment of Australian values and attitudes towards the first peoples of this continent. The revolutionary impulse implicit in Albrecht and his belief in an Aboriginal future is further underlined by the fact that Aboriginal futurism has only emerged as a theme of scholarly interest within Indigenous Studies programs in the past five years.[18]

Albrecht's belief in and commitment to an Aboriginal future ensured that the work he undertook as superintendent at Hermannsburg from his arrival in 1926 to his relocation to Alice Springs in 1952 would focus as much on secular issues of well-being and work as much as the religious imperative of converting the Aranda, Luritja and Pitjantjatjara to Lutheranism. In this secular work, which missionaries and pastors might designate 'pastoral care,' we argue Albrecht was not only influenced

The 'Problem of Work' 53

and directed by his Lutheranism but also by many of the key ideas that emerged during the eighteenth-century German Enlightenment and which, by the time of Albrecht, had become embedded in German culture and were influential in shaping German attitudes, values and understanding of the world. As we have already discussed, from Herder Albrecht accepted the central importance of culture in shaping the world and the relative value and worth of each culture in and of itself. From Hegel, he accepted that human progress and advancement occurs within the frame of history and is shaped by local culture, language and environment. In the various schemes he devised and then trialled to advance Aboriginal futures through education, training and employment, Albrecht not only gained inspiration from his Lutheran theology but also from the Kantian ideas that emphasised freedom and autonomy, personal responsibility and duty to self and others.

Almost immediately after his arrival at Hermannsburg, Albrecht was compelled to address secular issues that were adversely impacting the well-being of Aranda people as well as the ongoing viability of the Finke River Mission itself. He had arrived in Central Australia at the beginning of a severe period of drought, one that in the period 1927–1929 would cause scurvy among the Aranda converts at Hermannsburg as well as the loss of most of the mission stock.[19] Scurvy, the result of a lack of vitamin C, led to an exceptionally high rate of infant mortality, with around 85 per cent of all babies born in these years dying.[20] The disease had occurred in a Central Australian landscape that had been changed by the introduction of exotic species, such as cattle, sheep and goats, with many traditional plant-based food sources consequently eaten out and no longer available to support Aboriginal people. Albrecht thought the solution to this problem rightly rested in the ability of the mission to grow fresh fruit and vegetables on site. Yet when he arrived in 1926, the mission did not have immediate access to permanent sources of water. While the mission was situated on the north bank of the Finke River (or Larapinta in Aranda), the usual state of the river was dry. The only reliable source of water was situated at the Kuprilya Springs, located some 8 kms distance from the mission. Albrecht's first great work in support of Aboriginal futures was to raise money for the construction of a pipeline from Kuprilya to the mission.[21] In the first real test of his leadership skills, Albrecht was able to prove himself an effective communicator. Through several written pieces, he was able to convince the Lutheran clergy and many in their congregations to provide financial support for his pipeline project. Through a collaboration with the Melbourne-based artist Violet Teague and her sister Una, funds for the pipeline works were successfully raised through public subscription in South Australia and Victoria.[22] Built with labour provided by Aranda men, the pipeline from Kuprilya Springs was completed on 30 September 1935, with water flowing into the holding tank at the mission

54 *Barry Judd*

for the first time the next day. The holding tank, although unable to meet all requirements for water, provided enough to make gardens possible.

Reliable water and adequate supplies of fresh fruit and vegetables assured, the child mortality rate amongst the Aranda people at Hermannsburg dropped significantly. In finding a workable solution to the problem of scurvy brought about by years of drought, Albrecht not only proved his skills in leadership and persuasion to Lutheran congregations and the publics of the southern states but, importantly, his ability to improve the lot of Aranda people was also noticed by the Aranda themselves. As one of his Aboriginal converts noted: 'When we saw that one, the water, we said, old man, your word is really true. I'll get it, he said. He did! Pastor Albrecht's word was true altogether.'[23] The building of the Kuprilya pipeline continues to be remembered at Hermannsburg/Ntaria today, with an annual Kuprilya Day. In 1935, Albrecht led the people in prayers of thanksgiving when the water flowed and '[n]ow, every year on the first Sunday in October, the people of Hermannsburg gather at Kuprilya Spring for a thanksgiving day.'[24] Not only did the drought and the construction of the pipeline demonstrate the commitment of Albrecht to securing Aboriginal futures it also likely gave him insight into the capacity of Aboriginal men at the mission to work and to learn new skills useful to the workings of both the mission and the regional economy of Central Australia. Albrecht was certainly no businessman, but he understood that Aboriginal futures would require that the Aranda and other Aboriginal peoples become integrated in the national settler-colonial economy, and indeed the global economic systems of capitalism. The experience of Aboriginal labour that the Kuprilya pipeline project provided inspired Albrecht to find new and innovative schemes to put the Aranda people to work in ways that would both acculturate them to the workings of capitalist labour markets and progress the operations of the Finke River Mission to a situation of self-sufficiency.[25] The emphasis Albrecht placed on the economic integration of Aranda people confirms that he had no issue with assimilation, and in this respect he found himself in general agreement with the more progressive elements of the settler-colonial state who also advocated policies that were assimilationist in nature.[26] Yet there were significant differences between Albrecht's approach to assimilation and those pursued by the Australian state and non-Lutheran Churches and their missions to Aboriginal people. Albrecht held a qualified view of assimilation, holding that it was only good and only right when it occurred with the consent of Aboriginal people themselves.[27] That Albrecht placed this small but important caveat on assimilation in respect of Aboriginal people is described at length in later chapters when we discuss his scheme to educate "half-caste" children during the later part of his working life from the mid-1950s to the early 1960s. Yet an emphasis on the idea of consent is evident during his time as superintendent

The 'Problem of Work' 55

of Hermannsburg and the employment schemes he devised in the years following successful constructions of the pipeline.

Pathways to Economic Freedom and Cultural Autonomy

One of Albrecht's earliest and least successful schemes to create training and employment opportunities for Aranda people was a brush-making enterprise. The scheme was designed to make use of hair from the mission horses and recycle wood from packing crates to make brushes. Yet the work involved in brush making was found to be extremely tedious by the people Albrecht recruited to the scheme and enthusiasm for the work soon waned.[28] Moreover, Albrecht had done little to investigate market demand for horse hair brushes and when consignments of the product were sent to Lutheran congregations in South Australia they were met with underwhelming interest.[29] In working to create training and employment opportunities for Aranda converts at Hermannsburg, Albrecht also became increasing aware of the cultural complexities that impacted Aboriginal employment in Central Australia.

In this period Albrecht focussed his attention primarily on the training of men, finding them appropriate employment of use to themselves and their families and to the viability and self-sustainability of the Finke River Mission. Yet during his early trials of placing Aranda men in paid employment, he became acutely aware of how the local cultural values and the practice of resource sharing acted as a significant disincentive to the sacrifice in time and effort individuals might make in committing to paid labour. Albrecht noted that

> a worker on receiving his wages for four weeks work would purchase a 150lb bag of flour, as well as tea and sugar and return to his camp. Within a few days, all his real and tribal relatives would come and claim their share. Soon little remained for the weeks ahead until further wages were received. On several occasions women came to our door saying they were exhausted and could not continue because they had nothing to eat.[30]

The practice of sharing resources had been effective when Aranda and their near neighbours the Luritja and Pitjantjantjara had worked according to the economics of hunting and gathering. In these classical economies of Central Australia, the practice of resource sharing was the most effective way to ensure the physical well-being of family and kin for people who lived in the harshness of the arid interior of the continent. In these economies, immediate consumption was the necessary norm as all food (with the exception of grain) needed to be eaten soon after it was

56 *Barry Judd*

killed (kangaroo, emu, goanna etc.) or gathered (honey ant, native plum and onions etc.).[31] The economic idea of delaying consumption today (savings) to support consumption at some later time (the future) was a principle unknown to the Aboriginal peoples of Central Australia. The cultural principle of resource sharing, combined with a lack of insight into the economic idea of savings, was at the heart of the problems that the employment and training schemes Albrecht had devised encountered.[32] The application of these classical Aboriginal economic practices in the context of a capitalist, money-based national and global economic system resulted in a corrupted form of resource sharing that Albrecht noted in the quote above. Known as 'humbug,' the issue continues to be a problematic impediment to Aboriginal employment throughout Australia, and particularly in remote areas like Central Australia. These economic issues that Albrecht first became aware of during the late 1920s and early 1930s remain unresolved, and have been a major theme of the lifework of another significant Lutheran thinker, orator and doer, Noel Pearson of Cape York.[33]

The issue of humbug, and of the conflicting economic ideas that lay at its base, was one that Albrecht most famously came to confront through the training and support of the most famous and widely acclaimed Aranda person to ever have lived, the artist Albert (Elea) Namatjira (1902–1959).[34] Born at Hermannsburg and baptised into the Lutheran faith as an infant, Namatjira attended the mission school and resided at the boys dormitory until the age of 12 or 13. He then spent six months in the bush as a participant in initiation ceremony to become a man. As a young man, he worked as a stockman, cameleer, carpenter and blacksmith in the mission workshops for rations and on neighbouring pastoral stations for wages. During this time, he would make sketches of the men working the stock in the yards and he also began to produce wooden artefacts, boomerangs and woomeras. Seeing his interest in traditional 'crafts,' Albrecht encouraged him to develop his artistic skills through poker-worked designs on wood.[35] In 1932 and again in 1934, Rex Battarbee (like Albrecht a veteran of World War I), a local of South West Victoria, visited Hermannsburg to paint landscapes in watercolour.[36] The paintings he produced during his 1934 visit piqued Namatjira's interest in this artform and he repeatedly began to ask Albrecht for supplies of paints, brushes and paper. Albrecht eventually agreed on the condition that Namatjira would accompany Battarbee on his 1936 visit as a guide and cameleer. In return, Battarbee would train Namatjira to paint in watercolour with art supplies Albrecht purchased. Namatjira learned fast and the works he produced for his Country soon surpassed those of his teacher. In 1938, Battarbee arranged an exhibition of Albert's works in Melbourne at which all his works were sold.[37] By the 1950s, Namatjira had achieved widespread acclaim and national fame. Albrecht

The 'Problem of Work' 57

played a critical role in Albert's success – effectively acting as his agent and promoter.[38] As a working artist, Namatjira earned a sizable income and was able to access resources other Aranda people could not. After he was granted citizenship rights in 1957, his life took a turn for the worse as the gap between Aranda cultural expectations for sharing resources and his position as a successful working artist in the world of global capitalist economics collided. Namatjira became the constant target of humbugging by family and kin relations.[39] As Namatjira's income grew, so did his extended family. At one time he was singlehandedly providing over 600 people with financial support. These cultural obligations conflicted with settler-colonial law when he supplied 'family' with alcohol. When Pitjantjatjara woman, Fay Iowa, was killed at Morris Soak, Namatjira was held responsible by stipendiary magistrate, Jim Lemaire. He was convicted of an offence under the *Welfare Ordinance 1953 (NT)*, for supplying an Aboriginal person who under this legislation was regarded as a 'ward' of the state with liquor. Initially sentenced to six months in prison, after appeal and public uproar, the Minister for Territories, Paul Hasluck, intervened and the sentence was served at Papunya Native Reserve 250 kilometres northwest of Alice Springs.[40] He served only two months due to medical reasons.

The rise and subsequent fall of the artist Albert Namatjira occurred through the conflict of values and expectations created when Aranda men earned money through paid employment and then had the rewards of their individual initiative taken away by the corrupted cultural practice of resource sharing which now functioned as humbug. It was a lesson in cultural conflict that Albrecht was never quite able to fully reconcile, although it reinforced his belief that the future of the Aranda rested on their integration into the national and global capitalist economy as active and independent participants. The 'problem of work' that Albrecht became aware of through his growing understanding of Aranda cultural values and practices, and which was exemplified in the case of Albert Namatjira. Through Namatjira, Albrecht pursued his hopes and commitment to secure an Aboriginal future via pathways of training and employment but found these constantly mediated by bouts of despair and frustration that arose in the incommensurability of classical economic values that clashed with those the Aranda now required for success in the economics of national and global capitalism. Austin-Broos explains these hopes and frustrations in the following terms:

> Albrecht had some cultural insight nurtured by decades spent with Western Arrernte. His commitment to promoting work and apprenticeship showed some ambivalence, and was interspersed with cries of frustration. These are evident in his papers and in his biography. Henson observes that '[Albrecht's] efforts for economic progress were often undercut by recurring problems about work.'[41] Albrecht

58 *Barry Judd*

saw two main issues. One was the difficult relation between work and the authority of ritual life...The second issue that Albrecht identified was a supposed economy of limited good in which the meanings of commodities and cash, and time-space of Aboriginal life, were markedly at variance.[42]

Namatjira had proved beyond all doubt that Aranda men possessed the talent, capability and work ethic to be successful in the settler-colonial economy. His rise to national prominence had coincided with the development of another of Albrecht's training and employment schemes devised to facilitate both Aranda integration into the economics of capitalism and to create a commercial business opportunity whose profitability might support the viability and growth of the Finke River Mission. This scheme centred on the development of a tannery at the mission, a scheme that underlines the intent of his brand of assimilation, which was largely economic in nature. As Austin-Broos put it:

> Albrecht had sought to turn Hermannsburg into a rural industrial village following the disastrous drought of 1928–1929. He saw clearly that a hunting and foraging life was finished for the Arrernte and had himself played a part in disrupting 'nomadism.' He was therefore an early, committed, assimilationist.[43]

Unlike his earlier failed attempt to create industry through brush making, Albrecht's efforts to create training and employment for Aranda men proved to be much more successful in his scheme to develop a working tannery.[44] For some time, the mission had purchased kangaroo skins from Aranda people and sent these south for commercial sale in Adelaide. Seeking to build on this foundation, Albrecht believed that the skins could be processed on site at Hermannsburg. Again, Albrecht proved himself to be no businessman and the idea was set in train with little knowledge of the processes required. As a result, early attempts to tan cattle hides failed. However, after much trial and error the tanning process was mastered and a dedicated tannery was built in 1941. It proved a success. In addition to training in the tanning process, the Aranda men were also trained in leather work. They became skilled makers of whips, bridles, belts and similar articles that were then put up for sale on the open market. For several decades, the mission was able to supply all its own needs in leather and leather goods. So successful was the tannery scheme that extensions made in 1962 effectively doubled its size. Albrecht, always keen to add value to mission made products, also decided to try boot making. He sent one skilled Aranda man, Manasse, south for training with the famed Australian bootmaker R.M. Williams in his workshops in Adelaide. When

Manasse returned to Hermannsburg he taught others, and they began making blucher boots for use by local men (Figure 2.1).[45]

The development of a tannery operation at Hermannsburg underlines Albrecht's commitment to Aranda futures through their economic integration into the national and global economics of capitalism. The tannery, more than any of his other training and employment schemes, demonstrates Albrecht's efforts to transform Hermannsburg from a consumer of goods and services imported from the distant settled districts of South Australia to a producer and exporter of locally made goods and services. In the 1930s and 1940s this was an ambitious plan for Central Australia, one that remains so in the twenty-first century as the problems of economic development beyond the Stuart Highway zone and of employment in remote Aboriginal communities continues to vex Australian governments (Figure 2.2).[46]

If the brush making and the tannery schemes represented Albrecht's vision of an Aranda future based on a 'modern' industrialised future in a global capitalist economic system, another of his ideas sought to harness Aranda connection and knowledge of their Country. Perhaps drawing on his own childhood and youth spent as a farmer's son and his close connections to the Old Lutheran farming communities of South Australia, western Victoria, and the Riverina in New South Wales, Albrecht also conceived that Aranda futures would remain connected to the Aranda

Figure 2.1 'Making boots.' Courtesy of the Lutheran Archives.

Figure 2.2 'Tanning Time.' Courtesy of the Lutheran Archives.

past through a continued relationship with their traditional homelands. To this end, he trialled small land holdings based on family groupings, whereby men could work the land and earn a living to support their wives, children, and parents. Again Namatjira and his family became the test case.[47] However, here Albrecht encountered the same problems that had frustrated him in his industrial training and employment schemes. The Aranda economic principle of resource sharing, now corrupted by settler-colonial capitalist and money-based economics into the ritualised form of begging known as humbugging, once again undid the hope Albrecht held for a prosperous and independent Aranda future.[48] Despite this failure, the particular scheme Albrecht devised pointed to the homelands movement that would characterise the Aboriginal movement of self-determination in the Northern Territory during the 1970s following the granting of Land Rights.[49]

Anglo-Australians who recall Albrecht's efforts are likely to do so solely through the prism of settler-colonial assimilation policies of the Australian state and therefore wrongly characterised him with the derogatory label 'assimilationist.'[50] Few recognise that his brand of assimilation was always qualified by the requirement for consent. Fewer still have considered the ways in which concepts such as freedom, autonomy and personal responsibility, those ideas that can be traced to the age of German Enlightenment, framed the relationship Albrecht forged with

The 'Problem of Work' 61

Aranda and other Aboriginal peoples in Central Australia. Throughout this book we argue that these ideas of freedom, autonomy and responsibility almost never applied to Aboriginal peoples and their engagement with Christian mission or settler-colonial Anglo-Australian government are the central but overlooked concepts that framed the mission work of F. W. Albrecht. They are ideas that should be considered fundamental to contemporary assessments of his legacy and the broader legacy of the Finke River Mission. Few historians working in the field of 'Aboriginal history' have understood that assimilation, or acculturation to use a sociological term, is not in itself an evil. Indeed, many of these authors would do well to read Stuart Hall in order to understand that culture is forever in a dynamic state of flux, a struggle between tradition on the one hand and innovation and change on the other.[51] The simple proposition that F. W. Albrecht put forward to us is that cultural change is not in and of itself a bad thing. When cultural change occurs with the consent of those involved and exists as the outcome of freedom, autonomy and personal responsibility it should be regarded as valid and the choices made by the individuals, families and communities involved respected. As we will make clear in later chapters, to confuse advocacy for consensual assimilation with the Stolen Generations is to do Albrecht and the Old Lutheran clergy and congregations that supported him over decades a great disservice.

In the aftermath of the Finke River Mission era and the administration of race relations in Central Australia led by German-born men like F. W. Albrecht who advocated assimilation by consent and who focussed much of his time and attention in solving the very practical real-world problems of Aranda training and employment came the disappointing era of Australian government oversight. Gone was the Old Lutheran commitment from God to engage and respect the vernacular language and culture of the Aranda, Luritja and Pitjantjatjara. This was replaced with a commitment to interactions only through English, framed by the false understanding that Aborigines across the continent represent a homogenous group with the same needs, hopes, aspirations, cultural outlook and values. Gone too was the German world view that took the *Volk* seriously and that treated the Aranda and other Aboriginal peoples with respect and accepted their inherent ability to act as human agents and find freedom, autonomy and personal responsibility through faith, culture and reason. What replaced these forms of respect that derived from both Lutheran theology and some of the fundamental ideas of the German Enlightenment was an Australian government largely driven by the 'common-sense' misconceptions of settler-colonial Anglo-Australia based on forms of long-discredited biological racism, social Darwinism and the science of eugenics. Treated as children who lacked any agency, Aboriginal people were seen as museum pieces and curiosities; deliberately

62   Barry Judd

locked out of the national and global systems of capitalist economics. For the Australian government, and perhaps an overwhelming number of settler-colonial Anglo-Australians, the Enlightenment ideals of culture, history, progress, autonomy, reason, freedom, responsibility and duty do not apply to Aborigines. In Central Australia, the Australian government has all but given up on finding solutions to the issues of Aboriginal training and employment. The need to solve these issues makes remembrance of F. W. Albrecht and a discussion of what ideas, religious and cultural traditions motivated him to see the 'problem of work' at the very centre of his mission to the Aranda people at Hermannsburg a worthwhile project.

In the chapters that follow, we will trace how Albrecht's efforts to integrate Aboriginal peoples from Central Australia into the national and global economic system of capitalism led him to focus his efforts on children and a tough love program of assimilation. Through formal schooling that compelled children to distance themselves from their own cultures by boarding off Country, Albrecht believed he could transition successful pupils into meaningful 'mainstream' work. Importantly, this educational scheme that was unashamedly assimilationist by design was based on Aboriginal consent and agency and did not facilitate the forced removal of Aboriginal children from their families.

Notes

1 *Supplement to the London Gazette of 12 June 1958*, Issue 41405, 3 June 1958, 3551, https://www.thegazette.co.uk/London/issue/41405/supplement/3551, accessed 4 February 2023.
2 Barbara Henson, *A Straight-Out Man: F.W. Albrecht and Central Australian Aborigines* (Parkville: Melbourne University Press, 1992), 33, 57, 224.
3 Maurice Schild, 'Albrecht, Friedrich Wilhelm (1894–1984),' in *Australian Dictionary of Biography*, National Centre of Biography, Australian National University, https://adb.anu.edu.au/biography/albrecht-friedrich-wilhelm-12126/text21725, published first in hardcopy 2007, accessed online 4 February 2023.
4 Schild, 'Albrecht, Friedrich Wilhelm.'
5 For details of Strehlow's life and work see Walter F. Veit, 'Strehlow, Carl Friedrich (1871–1922),' in *Australian Dictionary of Biography*, National Centre of Biography, Australian National University, https://adb.anu.edu.au/biography/strehlow-carl-friedrich-8698/text15221, published first in hardcopy 1990, accessed online 29 January 2023.
6 Schild, 'Albrecht, Friedrich Wilhelm.'
7 Henson, *A Straight-Out Man*, 2–6.
8 Henson, *A Straight-Out Man*, 224, 231.
9 Henson, *A Straight-Out Man*, 33.
10 Sonia Sikka, *Herder on Humanity and Cultural Difference: Enlightened Relativism* (Cambridge: Cambridge University Press, 2012).
11 See H. J. Hillerbrand, 'Martin Luther,' *Encyclopedia Britannica*, 4 January 2023, https://www.britannica.com/biography/Martin-Luther, accessed 29 January 2023; David Moore, 'The Reformation, Lutheran tradition, and missionary linguistics,' in 'German Lutheran Missionaries and the linguistic description of

The 'Problem of Work' 63

Central Australian languages, 1890–1910' (PhD Thesis: University of Western Australia, 2019), 21–38. On Albrecht's commitment to teaching the Scripture in Aranda, see Henson, *A Straight-Out Man*, 29.

12 Paul G. E. Albrecht, 'The Finke River Mission Approach to Mission Work among Aborigines in Central Australia,' *Lutheran Theological Journal* 32, No. 1 (1998): 7–15.

13 Henson, *A Straight-Out Man*, 110–111, 126, 149–150.

14 Patrick Wolfe, 'Settler Colonialism and the Elimination of the Native,' *Journal of Genocide Research* 8, No. 4 (2006): 387–409; Patrick Wolfe, *Settler Colonialism and the Transformation of Anthropology: The Politics and Poetics of an Ethnographic event* (London; New York: Cassell, 1999).

15 For a discussion of the doomed race theory in Australia, see Russell McGregor, *Imagined Destinies: Aboriginal Australians and the Doomed Race Theory, 1880–1939* (Carlton: Melbourne University Press, 1997).

16 Anna Haebich, *Spinning the Dream: Assimilation in Australia 1950–1970* (North Fremantle: Fremantle Press, 2008).

17 Henson, *A Straight-Out Man*, 223–241.

18 P. Vijayasekaran and G. Alan, 'The Future of Colonialism in Australian Indigenous Fiction–A Psychoanalytic Study of Trauma in The Swan Book and Terra Nullius,' *Theory and Practice in Language Studies* 12, No. 8 (2022): 1664–1668; Liubica Matek, 'Australian Aboriginal SF–Blending Genre and Literary Fiction: A Review of Futuristic Worlds in Australian Aboriginal Fiction by Iva Polak,' *ELOPE: English Language Overseas Perspectives and Enquiries* 15, No. 1 (2018): 129–131; Sean Guynes, 'Indigenous Futurism,' *American Book Review* 41, No. 1 (2019): 6. https://doi.org/10.1353/abr.2019.0124.

19 Henson, *A Straight-Out Man*, 15–38.

20 'Kuprilya Springs Pipeline and Tank,' Hermannsburg Historic Precinct, https://hermannsburg.com.au/stories/kuprilya-springs-pipeline, accessed 12 February 2023.

21 Henson, *A Straight-Out Man*, 77–96.

22 Henson, *A Straight-Out Man*, 85–86.

23 Henson, *A Straight-Out Man*, 96.

24 Neville Doecke, 'Kwatja, Kwatja! Kuprilya Day 2020,' Finke River Mission, 15 October 2020, https://finkerivermission.lca.org.au/kwatja-kwatja-kuprilya-day-2020/, accessed 13 February 2023.

25 Paul G. E. Albrecht, 'The Reflections of a Reluctant Missionary,' *Journal of Friends of Lutheran Archives* 28 (2018): 37–51, https://search.informit.org/doi/10.3316/informit.396869359644988, accessed 12 January 2023.

26 John Chesterman and Heather Douglas, '"Their ultimate absorption": Assimilation in 1930s Australia,' *Journal of Australian Studies* 28, No. 81 (2004): 47–58; Catriona Elder, *Dreams and Nightmares of a White Australia: Representing Aboriginal Assimilation in the Mid-Twentieth Century*, Vol. 3 (Bern: Peter Lang, 2009).

27 See Paul G. E. Albrecht, *From Mission to Church, 1877–2002: Finke River Mission* (Hermannsburg: Finke River Mission, 2002).

28 Henson, *A Straight-Out Man*, 36.

29 F. Everard Leske, ed., M. Lohe, F. W. Albrecht, L. H. Leske (contributing authors), *Hermannsburg: A Vision and a Mission*, revised ed. (Adelaide: Lutheran Publishing House, 2016), 44.

30 Albrecht in Leske, ed., *Hermannsburg*, 43.

31 For a discussion of these issues see Tim Rowse, *White Flour, White Power: From Rations to Citizenship in Central Australia* (Cambridge; Melbourne: Cambridge University Press, 1998).

64 *Barry Judd*

32 Diane Austin-Broos, '"Working for" and "Working" among Western Arrernte in Central Australia,' *Oceania* 76, No. 1 (March 2006): 1–3.

33 Noel Pearson, *Mission: Essays, Speeches and Ideas* (Carlton: Black Inc., 2021); Noel Pearson, *Our Right to Take Responsibility* (Cairns: Noel Pearson and Associates, 2000).

34 Sylvia Kleinert, 'Namatjira, Albert (Elea) (1902–1959),' in *Australian Dictionary of Biography*, National Centre of Biography, Australian National University, https://adb.anu.edu.au/biography/namatjira-albert-elea-11217/text19999, published first in hardcopy 2000, accessed online 12 February 2023.

35 Henson, *A Straight-Out Man*, 74–75, 206.

36 On Rex Battarbee, see Jane Hardy, 'Battarbee, Reginald Ernest (Rex) (1893–1973),' in *Australian Dictionary of Biography*, National Centre of Biography, Australian National University, https://adb.anu.edu.au/biography/battarbee-reginald-ernest-rex-9453/text16625, published first in hardcopy 1993, accessed online 12 February 2023.

37 On Battarbee's organisation of the exhibition, see Steve Meacham, 'Albert Namatjira 80 Years On: The Untold Story Behind His First Exhibition,' *Australian Financial Review*, 9 February 2018, https://www.afr.com/life-and-luxury/arts-and-culture/albert-namatjira-80-years-on-the-untold-story-behind-his-first-exhibition-20180207-h0v7qz, accessed 12 February 2023.

38 Kleinert, 'Namatjira, Albert.' For an account of Namatjira's gratitude for Albrecht's work, see Henson, *A Straight-Out Man*, 206.

39 Henson, *A Straight-Out Man*, 233–235.

40 Kleinert, 'Namatjira, Albert.'

41 Henson, *A Straight-Out Man*, 111.

42 Austin-Broos, '"Working for" and "Working" among Western Arrernte in Central Australia,' 2.

43 Austin-Broos, '"Working for" and "Working" among Western Arrernte in Central Australia,' 2.

44 'Skins, Leather and Industry at Hermannsburg,' Hermannsburg Historic Precinct, https://hermannsburg.com.au/stories/working-at-the-tannery, accessed 12 February 2023; Henson, *A Straight-Out Man*, 110–111, 123, 133, 282.

45 Albrecht in Leske, ed., *Hermannsburg*, 68–69.

46 Tim Rowse, *White Flour, White Power*; Dean Carson, 'Political Economy, Demography and Development in Australia's Northern Territory,' *The Canadian Geographer/Le Géographe Canadien* 55, No. 2 (2011): 226–242.

47 Henson, A Straight-Out Man, 198.

48 Austin-Broos, '"Working for" and "Working" among Western Arrernte in Central Australia,' 2.

49 For Albrecht's views on Aboriginal rights to land, see Henson, *A Straight-Out Man*, 89–90, 108, 131–132, 271.

50 Austin-Broos, '"Working for" and "Working" among Western Arrernte in Central Australia,' 1.

51 Stuart Hall, 'Culture, Community, Nation,' *Cultural Studies* 7, No. 3 (1993): 349–363; Mark Alizart, Dir., *Stuart Hall* (Éditions Amsterdam, 2007); Stuart Hall and Paul Du Gay, eds. *Questions of Cultural Identity* (London: Sage, 1996).

Bibliography

Primary

Doecke, Neville. 'Kwatja, Kwatja! Kuprilya Day 2020.' Finke River Mission, 15 October 2020. https://finkerivermission.lca.org.au/kwatja-kwatja-kuprilya-day-2020/, accessed 13 February 2023.

The 'Problem of Work'   65

Supplement to the London Gazette of 12 June 1958. Issue 41405, 3 June 1958, 3551, https://www.thegazette.co.uk/London/issue/41405/supplement/3551, accessed 4 February 2023.

Secondary

Albrecht, Paul G. E. *From Mission to Church, 1877–2002: Finke River Mission.* Hermannsburg: Finke River Mission, 2002.

Albrecht, Paul G. E. 'The Finke River Mission Approach to Mission Work among Aborigines in Central Australia.' *Lutheran Theological Journal* 32, Number 1 (1998): 7–15.

Albrecht, Paul G. E. 'The Reflections of a Reluctant Missionary.' *Journal of Friends of Lutheran Archives* 28 (2018): 37–51, https://search.informit.org/doi/10.3316/informit.396869359644988, accessed 12 January 2023.

Alizart, Mark. Director. *Stuart Hall.* Éditions Amsterdam, 2007.

Austin-Broos, Diane. '"Working for" and "Working" among Western Arrernte in Central Australia.' *Oceania* 76, Number 1 (March 2006): 1–15.

Carson, Dean. 'Political Economy, Demography and Development in Australia's Northern Territory.' *The Canadian Geographer/Le Géographe Canadien* 55, Number 2 (2011): 226–242.

Chesterman, John and Heather Douglas. '"Their ultimate absorption": Assimilation in 1930s Australia.' *Journal of Australian Studies* 28, Number 81 (2004): 47–58.

Elder, Catriona. *Dreams and Nightmares of a White Australia: Representing Aboriginal Assimilation in the Mid-Twentieth Century.* Volume 3. Bern: Peter Lang, 2009.

Guynes, Sean. 'Indigenous Futurism.' *American Book Review* 41, Number 1 (2019): 6. https://doi.org/10.1353/abr.2019.0124

Haebich, Anna. *Spinning the Dream: Assimilation in Australia 1950–1970.* North Fremantle: Fremantle Press, 2008.

Hall, Stuart. 'Culture, Community, Nation.' *Cultural Studies* 7, Number 3 (1993): 349–363.

Hall, Stuart and Paul Du Gay, editors. *Questions of Cultural Identity.* London: Sage, 1996.

Hardy, Jane. 'Battarbee, Reginald Ernest (Rex) (1893–1973).' In *Australian Dictionary of Biography,* National Centre of Biography, Australian National University, https://adb.anu.edu.au/biography/battarbee-reginald-ernest-rex-9453/text16625, published first in hardcopy 1993, accessed online 15 February 2023.

Henson, Barbara. *A Straight-Out Man: F. W. Albrecht and Central Australian Aborigines.* Parkville: Melbourne University Press, 1992.

Hillerbrand, Hans J. 'Martin Luther.' In *Encyclopedia Britannica.* 4 January 2023. https://www.britannica.com/biography/Martin-Luther, accessed 29 January 2023.

Kleinert, Sylvia. 'Namatjira, Albert (Elea) (1902–1959).' In *Australian Dictionary of Biography,* National Centre of Biography, Australian National University, https://adb.anu.edu.au/biography/namatjira-albert-elea-11217/text19999, published first in hardcopy 2000, accessed online 12 February 2023.

'Kuprilya Springs Pipeline and Tank.' Hermannsburg Historic Precinct, https://hermannsburg.com.au/stories/kuprilya-springs-pipeline, accessed 12 February 2023.

66 Barry Judd

Leske, Everard, editor, M. Lohe, F. W. Albrecht and L. H. Leske (Contributing Authors). *Hermannsburg: A Vision and a Mission.* Revised edition. Adelaide: Lutheran Publishing House, 2016.

Matek, Liubica. 'Australian Aboriginal SF–Blending Genre and Literary Fiction: A Review of Futuristic Worlds in Australian Aboriginal Fiction by Iva Polak.' *ELOPE: English Language Overseas Perspectives and Enquiries* 15, Number 1 (2018): 129–131.

McGregor, Russell. *Imagined Destinies: Aboriginal Australians and the doomed race theory, 1880–1939.* Carlton: Melbourne University Press, 1997.

Meacham, Steve. 'Albert Namatjira 80 Years On: The Untold Story Behind his First Exhibition.' *Australian Financial Review*, 9 February 2018, https://www.afr.com/life-and-luxury/arts-and-culture/albert-namatjira-80-years-on-the-untold-story-behind-his-first-exhibition-20180207-h0v7qz, accessed 12 February 2023.

Moore, David. 'The Reformation, Lutheran Tradition, and Missionary Linguistics.' In 'German Lutheran Missionaries and the linguistic description of Central Australian languages, 1890–1910.' PhD Thesis: University of Western Australia, 2019.

Pearson, Noel. *Mission: Essays, Speeches and Ideas.* Carlton: Black Inc., 2021.

Pearson, Noel. *Our Right to Take Responsibility.* Cairns: Noel Pearson and Associates, 2000.

Rowse, Tim. *White Flour, White Power: From Rations to Citizenship in Central Australia.* Cambridge; Melbourne: Cambridge University Press, 1998.

Schild, Maurice. 'Albrecht, Friedrich Wilhelm (1894–1984).' *Australian Dictionary of Biography*, National Centre of Biography, Australian National University, https://adb.anu.edu.au/biography/albrecht-friedrich-wilhelm-12126/text21725, published first in hardcopy 2007, accessed online 4 February 2023.

Sikka, Sonia. *Herder on Humanity and Cultural Difference: Enlightened Relativism.* Cambridge: Cambridge University Press, 2012.

'Skins, Leather and Industry at Hermannsburg,' Hermannsburg Historic Precinct, https://hermannsburg.com.au/stories/working-at-the-tannery, accessed 12 February 2023.

Veit, Walter F. 'Strehlow, Carl Friedrich (1871–1922).' In *Australian Dictionary of Biography*, National Centre of Biography, Australian National University, https://adb.anu.edu.au/biography/strehlow-carl-friedrich-8698/text15221, published first in hardcopy 1990, accessed online 29 January 2023.

Vijayasekaran, P. and G. Alan. 'The Future of Colonialism in Australian Indigenous Fiction–A Psychoanalytic Study of Trauma in the Swan Book and Terra Nullius.' *Theory and Practice in Language Studies* 12, Number 8 (2022): 1664–1668.

Wolfe, Patrick. 'Settler Colonialism and the Elimination of the Native.' *Journal of Genocide Research* 8, Number 4 (2006): 387–409.

Wolfe, Patrick. *Settler Colonialism and the Transformation of Anthropology: The Politics and Poetics of an Ethnographic Event.* London; New York: Cassell, 1999.

3 Mparntwe and the Mission Block

Albrecht's Education Scheme for Aboriginal Girls

Katherine Ellinghaus

After nearly 30 years of work at Ntaria (Hermannsburg), F.W. Albrecht and his wife, Minna, moved to Mparntwe (Alice Springs) following a year-long trip back to Germany to visit family, attend mission festivals and spend a week in London. Pastor S. O. Gross became the superintendent at Hermannsburg, leaving Albrecht to focus on building a new life of service in Mparntwe. Mparntwe is on Aranda land, but since the very early days of the twentieth century, Anangu people from a variety of language groups gravitated to the town. These outsiders included the Larrakia, Kungarakan, Warlpiri, Warumungu, Gurindji, Pitjantjatjara, Luritja, Pintupi and even people from as far away as the Tiwi, Melville and Thursday Islands.

This chapter describes the period of Albrecht's work from 1952 when he moved to Mparntwe to care for Minna, who suffered regular periods of ill-health. During this time, Albrecht continued his mission work and expressed his ideas about individualism and religion through a scheme designed to offer choices and education to a small number of children who seemed, to either him or their parents, able to take advantage of such an opportunity. These ideas placed Albrecht in conflict with the Australian government and other Church bodies in terms of their ideas about who Aboriginal people should be and how they should behave. Albrecht's views, drawn from his Lutheran background and views about education, progress and humanity formed in nineteenth-century Europe, but also developed by his relationships with Anangu people, pushed back against the project of Aboriginal assimilation in post-World War II Australia. At this point in his life, Albrecht embodied the Enlightenment, both by his very presence in Mparntwe – bringing Christianity, reason and progress to the far reaches of the earth – but also in the views he held about the possibilities of all humans to reach their potential, and in the actions those views inspired.

In the 1950s the township of Mparntwe was growing, and many Anangu people lived there or visited regularly, working for the European

DOI: 10.4324/9781003281634-4

68 *Katherine Ellinghaus*

community or accessing the town's services and pleasures. The town itself was a place of tension, divided into spaces that were defined and bordered by the tensions of settler-colonialism.[1] The centre of town had been designated as a prohibited area in 1928, meaning that most Anangu people were technically guilty of an offence just by being there. Meanwhile, in 1952 local Administrators began lobbying the Territory government for funds to create more housing for 'non-wards,' and officials began discussing the pros and cons of creating segregated suburbs or 'pepper potting' Anangu families into European residential areas.[2] The town was small, but in its streets the conflicting European aims of assimilation and segregation were played out on an everyday basis.

The Mission Block

The Finke River Mission Block sat apart, somewhat, from these tensions. Back in 1938 the Lutherans had purchased a six-acre block of land on Gap Road. They held services under a gum tree (which still stands) until they managed to build a small stone Church. By 1952, the land featured that Church, as well as an old, corrugated-iron army barracks which served as accommodation for mission staff passing through, a recreation room, and a bush timber-framed building which served as a store. There was also accommodation for people coming into town from surrounding stations, an evangelists' home of a couple of rooms and a manse in which Albrecht and his family planned to live.[3]

When Albrecht arrived, the education of Anangu children in the town was already a source of tension.[4] In late February 1951, Anangu parents had protested police harassment by keeping their children home from school.[5] The schools were unofficially segregated. European education in Mparntwe had been patchily offered to Anangu children from 1914, when they were given a segregated education in the first school set up in the town by police officer Robert Stott in a corrugated iron shed near the police station.[6] In the 1950s, there were two primary schools in Mparntwe: one in Hartley Street where most of the white children in the town went and a school at the Bungalow which was an institution for Anangu children established in 1915. Hartley Street had been built in 1929, and in 1945 a new kindergarten and classroom were built which are now recognised by the National Trust. Alice Springs Higher primary school was opened near Anzac Hill in 1953, but there was no proper high school in the town until 1961. There were also two mission-run hostels that provided accommodation and some schooling for children from remote communities. The Australian Board of Missions operated St Mary's Hostel, which provided accommodation and schooling for Anangu children who were either sent by their parents to town for schooling or removed from their families and committed

Mparntwe and the Mission Block 69

to the Hostel by the Director of Native Affairs. St John's hostel was established in 1941 by the Church of England to provide educational opportunities for Anangu children who came to town for schooling. Outside the town, there were also mission-run schools for Aboriginal children at settlements and stations across the Northern Territory. The Finke River Mission *News Letter* of 1955 carefully detailed the growing school attendance in remote communities and particularly noted that it was parents driving the growth of these schools: 'From attendance figures mentioned above, it is obvious that the parents of Native children have become education conscious and are cooperating to the best they can.'[7]

Albrecht brought with him the Hermannsburg emphasis on education to Mparntwe, and quickly became involved in the issue of education of Anangu children in the town, particularly those beyond primary school age. He also maintained a watching brief on what was happening in the administration of Aboriginal Affairs in Darwin and in Canberra. It was a time of change, as new ideas about cultural assimilation engrossed Australian government administrators and flooded the public domain in what historian Anna Haebich calls the 'powerful act of national imagining' which allowed white Australians to envision both Indigenous people and immigrants disappearing into a culturally homogenous settler democracy.[8] On 17 March 1954, Albrecht wrote to the Director of Native Affairs in response to the Wards Employment Ordinance (1953), one of a slew of ordinances passed that year that signalled new efforts to assimilate and control Aboriginal people in the Territory.[9] This letter was the first time that Albrecht signalled his concerns about what would happen to Aboriginal boys and girls after they had finished the primary-level schooling that was all that was available in the Territory at the time. He wrote that the children, 'after they have left school, are left to their own devices with very bad results,' and suggested an apprenticeship scheme that would 'decisively' help '[t]hese growing boys and girls'.[10]

Accommodating and supporting children coming to town for education became a large part of Albrecht's mission. He gave them lifts in and out of town as he travelled in his truck back and forth from stations and settlements doing his mission work. In Mparntwe, Albrecht also ran a thriving Sunday School – by 1963 there were 80 children enrolled, and new rooms were built by the congregation at a cost of £2,144/13/6d. In 1963, two Cottages and three three-bedroom cottages were built on the Mission Block to cater for children coming in from remote cattle stations to attend school in town.[11] At the beginning of the 1964 school-year as the missionaries themselves described in 1977,

> each home, under the care of a house-mother, had twelve children. These were children raw from the bush, shyly ready to try life and

Figure 3.1 'Finke River Mission, NT, Alice Springs. The old church with its bell at the front. 1950s.' Courtesy of the Lutheran Archives.

learning in a European setting at the Alice Springs public school. It was a bold experiment which had the full cooperation of the parents.[12]

By 1967 there were 100 children enrolled in the classes held at the Church on Saturday mornings (Figure 3.1).

The missionaries tried to make the 'Mission Block' on Gap Road a patch of Mparntwe that provided an escape from violence and alcohol, as well as the racism of the town and settler society more widely. The missionaries saw the Mission Block as a place where people coming into town from remote stations and settlements could find a 'peaceful refuge from the drunken brawls in the bed of the Todd River and other unofficial camping places.' The block was literally fenced off during this period by a six-foot wire-mesh fence.[13] More practically, the Mission ran a cash store, 'built of bush timber and second-hand iron,' that stood near the entrance. This store provided an alternative place to purchase clothes, sweets and other goods to the shops in the centre of town, which were often not very welcoming, as well as a place to socialise and congregate (Figure 3.2).[14]

By the early 1960s, the congregation consisted of both Anangu and Europeans, and the services were conducted in English and Aranda. Writing in the 1970s, F. W. Albrecht and his co-authors M. Lohe and L. H. Leske described how at the Sunday school 'catechetical instructions were given to children of all races' and the Mission 'aimed at avoiding

Figure 3.2 'Alice Springs Lutheran Store, Mbanta'. (Mparntwe). Courtesy of the Lutheran Archives.

racial distinctions, and concentrated on providing its services both in the religious and social sphere on a linguistic basis.' Though the services were segregated, it was up to individuals as to 'which chapter of the congregation or its arms he or she attended.' This was in accord with Lutheran policy always to aim at ministering in the tongue of the people among whom it is privileged to serve.[15] Barbara Henson describes how in these years the 'Alice Springs congregation was steadily growing. Typically, the little Church was filled, with many others sitting on the ground outside the door and beneath the windows.'[16] Albrecht's Christmas letter from 1958 described a Christmas service given in Aranda which had over 300 people attending.[17]

There were times when the town pushed back against the efforts of the Mission to provide a safe, multicultural space. The missionaries ran into problems when trying to build homes for elderly Anangu people to live on the Mission Block. They were told their plan was

> not acceptable, because at that time no permit would be granted to build a home for [an Aboriginal person of full descent]. The Director of Lands made it clear that Alice Springs was to have no [Aboriginal people of full descent] as residents in its area.

After protracted negotiations, the mission was finally granted a Special Purpose Lease, and they still hold the land today.[18]

72 *Katherine Ellinghaus*

Albrecht's Education Scheme

With the missionaries doing their best to make the Mission Block a place of welcome, and a proportion of the Anangu community using it as a place of refuge, Albrecht became increasingly involved in the issue of children's education. He developed a small educational scheme, which we argue can be seen as an expression of the larger historical events and intellectual history described in the first two chapters. In 1955, Albrecht was corresponding with the Department of Native Affairs and the Education Department in Darwin. Still sitting in his files in the Lutheran Archives in Adelaide is a letter from L. Dodd, the Assistant Supervisor of Education, Northern Territory Schools about allowances for 'children who are compelled to live away from home'. Albrecht starred one of the paragraphs, and kept the letter – the paragraph described an increase and an 'important alteration' to the boarding allowance for primary and junior secondary children. The allowance was now available to students whose homes were more than ten miles from an established school in the Northern Territory or in any of the States. Previously this allowance was available only for children who attended a school in the Northern Territory.[19] That small asterisk is one of our first indications that Albrecht was also planning a scheme that would take junior secondary students to schools beyond the Territory.[20]

Over the next few years, Albrecht consolidated his ideas about education and became more convinced of the need to facilitate children to leave Mparntwe to be educated if they wished. In September of 1954, Albrecht again expressed his interest in finding a solution for the post-school training of Aboriginal children, this time by suggesting he send boys out of the Territory 'to learn a trade'. Albrecht wrote to Brother Zinnbauer, of the Lutheran City Mission in Adelaide suggesting they use his hostel for this purpose, and noting '[o]ur biggest obstacle will probably be finance.'[21] The idea of sending children south was not new: Albrecht was following the lead of other Church organisations in Mparntwe. The Australian Board of Missions had first sent children who had been living at the St Mary's Hostel to Adelaide in 1945. In 1946, they established St Francis House in Adelaide to house children sent from Central Australia.[22] In a 1956 letter, Albrecht described the crucial moment when children left school in their early teens. The boys, he said, were taken by the old men and put through initiation and then they returned to Mparntwe, where

> the very confusing influence of the pictures, the attractions in gambling and drink, just sweep them off their feet, and most of them just drift. At the same time, these boys, if taken out to a station, find themselves complete strangers. They don't like station life, with living

Mparntwe and the Mission Block 73

conditions they are not used to. Away from pictures, life seems dull. They have no love for the out back sort of life, riding all day, breaking in horses, making their own dampers, or trailing the dingo. The school, instead of fitting these boys for life, has done a lot of damage to them, has actually pauperised them.

The only alternative, Albrecht argued, was 'to lead these children from the earliest possible age, step by step, into this new way of life and train them into it.' Albrecht finished the letter by advocating compulsory apprenticeships, which he likened to an initiation process where 'others' (not the parents)

> ensure the boy had to go through a lot of suffering to make him realise he belonged to a society where he could not do as he liked, but had to comply with their requirements, submit to the authority of the elders etc.[23]

In 1957 he wrote to Rev. R.B. Reuther, the Chairman of the Board of Management of the Finke River Mission, about the 'tragedy' of the education Anangu children were receiving in Mparntwe schools. 'These children are estranged to their way of life,' he wrote, 'they no longer feel at home and happy in the bush, yet in towns they face their doom.' Albrecht mused about the possibility of a '"flying school", a teacher travelling in a caravan and teaching for some weeks or months at a time ... This would overcome illiteracy, at the same time not uproot them.'[24] A year later, Albrecht wrote again to Reuther about his worries for the children in Mparntwe:

> Here they live in an atmosphere of dirt and drink, and when they come to that critical age, others take advantage, and they are spoilt for a lifetime, whereas if they would be kept in a good home, helped in a practical way to learn how to run a house, do some cooking, and sewing, have contact with the Church there, and young people, I am sure this would be of decisive importance to them.

Albrecht continued to grapple with the issue of education in his work in the last years of the decade. In 1959 he wrote a submission to the Lutheran Board about the need for a Lutheran Hostel in Mparntwe. In this pamphlet, Albrecht did more than just lobby for the need for accommodation for the 'brilliant' Anangu children who might need to come to Mparntwe for high school education: he also introduced the idea of sending children South where they could be housed in 'Christian homes.' Albrecht spoke of his worry that if the mission simply provided accommodation for children older than primary school age who had 'left

74 *Katherine Ellinghaus*

school, are working in town, attend the High School, or are apprenticed' then, given 'the whole atmosphere and attitude in town,' the mission would be doing nothing other than 'breeding delinquents.'[25]

Meanwhile, Albrecht dealt with a steady stream of children coming to live at the Mission Block in order to access education. In 1960, he had '25 children attending school from our block, while living under conditions which are neither hygiene nor wholesome, but while they are there they are more or less our responsibility.'[26] He was deeply concerned that the schooling they received was inadequate and that the town itself was a bad influence, and was constantly working on solutions:

> The stage is reached here that I feel, if the Board wants to go against it, that I shall discontinue encouraging such children now living at cattle stations, to come into Alice Springs. I know only too well what happens to them here, the little schooling they are getting does not compensate for the dangers these children are exposed to. And if they come, then it will be a matter of standing by helplessly and look on. The school just cannot help these children to gain an attitude that will help them find their level in our community. At the same time, the old order of people just staying on at cattle stations, has passed and they have to try and find some corner where they will fit in. If not helped, then they just drift.[27]

At some point Albrecht began to see the dangers of the town as greater for girls. He thought it best for them to 'go South'. It is telling that Albrecht focussed on girls likely around the age of menarche, when they might become sexually active. He wanted to send them South 'at the age of about 12 …for 2 or 3 years.' '[T]hey would then know,' he wrote,

> what to do next: Either return here and join their parents, or else settle down to further study of domestic duties. Whatever such girls would choose, the way into life generally would be open to them, which in most cases would not have been the case had they stayed.[28]

A year earlier, in 1958, Albrecht told Reuther that he had four children, all girls, 'all keen, and the parents, too, [who] are keen to have them sent down'. 'I am sure,' he said, 'if our people in the South know about it, there will be some who will open their homes to them.'[29] Through the first half of 1958, Albrecht and Reuther tried to find willing families for each of the girls. Reuther was fully supportive of the scheme. 'This seems to be some form of assimilation which might work,' he wrote in October, 'at least it is a stepping stone.'[30] Things looked 'pretty grim' in December 1958 but then, finally, in January 1959 after a flurry of last-minute efforts they found families for all four girls.[31] The scheme had begun.

Mparntwe and the Mission Block 75

Albrecht's scheme was never strictly only for girls, even though in the end it was mostly girls who were sent South in the first decade the scheme was in operation. The connection between Enlightenment thinking and the rise of feminism in Europe from the seventeenth century has long been recognised, and here, in Mparntwe in the 1950s, Albrecht had no hesitation in leaning into the importance of education for Anangu girls.[32] Whether this was part of his personal philosophy about women's education, we cannot be sure. We do know that he insisted on his own daughters being well educated. As his biographer, Barbara Henson put it, Albrecht's

> own children had received a clear message throughout their childhood that they were free to choose any career for themselves. The idea of not training for anything was not even mentioned—education for one's walk in life was simply assumed, for girls equally as boys. He had not forgotten his early days at the Hermannsburg institute where he had been shocked to see young women working in households for next to nothing. Only education, he felt, could help women against this kind of injustice.[33]

It is also possible that Anangu parents came to him for help with their daughters. It is likely, too, that girls were more palatable to Christian families down South, especially given the common practice of Aboriginal girls working as domestic servants in white families across all Australian states and territories.[34]

A Co-Designed Scheme

Albrecht's ideas about education were formed not just in conversation with other Lutherans, or the interested do-gooders with whom he corresponded. His ideas also drew on the advocacy of the Anangu parents and children that he was in contact with on a day-to-day basis. With hindsight, we can see that Albrecht's ideas, though expressed with some harshness, turned out to be true: the maintenance of Central Australian remote communities have allowed Anangu to maintain culture and tradition. But the lack of support and infrastructure shown to them by successive Northern Territory governments, and their very remoteness, has meant that educational opportunities are limited. And this was not lost on Anangu parents. While government administrators and missionaries were discussing the 'problem' of Aboriginal education amongst themselves, in Mparntwe Anangu parents were advocating for their children and children were advocating for themselves. Many of them spoke to Albrecht, as well as to Acting Patrol Officer and later Welfare Officer William (Billy) McCoy and A. A. Pearce, the headmaster of the Higher Primary School in Mparntwe. This

76 Katherine Ellinghaus

meant that Albrecht's ideas about education swerved away from the idea that education should take place away from towns and into the development of a scheme which expressed the Enlightenment ideals of rationalism and self-improvement in ways that responded to the particular needs of the Anangu people he came into contact with every day.

Albrecht never wrote directly that he developed his educational scheme in response to parents' wishes, whether because he never recognised that or because he did not think his audience wanted to hear it. But while he was teasing out his views about Aboriginal education in his correspondence, there is evidence in the archive and in oral history that parents and children initiated and were fully involved in the plans to send their children south for schooling. In 1955, for example, Albrecht wrote about 'Natives who are growing more and more anxious to see their children educated, and for these it would be a tragedy if they had to move to a town or other centre to have this accomplished.'[35] In 1958, he told the Board of how in

> a number of instances when ... - Natives have asked our advice, we have told them to keep their children at the cattle station where they happen to work, instead of sending them in here. The little they gain by some formal education, is nothing compared with the damage the children sustain in a place like Alice Springs. To us it has been encouraging to see to what extent the ... parents see this point and act accordingly.[36]

Albrecht's submission to the Lutheran board mentioned that he was responding to 'quite a number of coloured families' who were 'conscious of the fact that their children have to be educated, otherwise it can happen that the Welfare Department steps in and removes [them].'[37]

The journey of one the first of Albrecht's students to go south, N. Garrett, was prompted by Albrecht getting to know her in his religious instruction classes. Albrecht's scheme unofficially began in 1954 with N. Garrett and her brother, who had been attending the Alice Springs Higher primary school and doing well with their education. After advocacy by their parents, Albrecht arranged for both children to go to South Australia. N. Garrett lived with the Kennedy family in Nurioopta, her brother in Keynton and both attended high school. According to Barbara Henson '[w]hen it became known around town that the ... children were going south to school, other part-Aboriginal parents spoke to him. Obviously, there were others who wanted their children to have wider opportunities.'[38] He wrote to her parents in 1953:

> My dear friends, your dear girlie ... gave me your address, and I am glad to be able to write to you these lines. ... Both [children] are

Mparntwe and the Mission Block 77

attending the religious instructions I have started here since after Christmas. … [N. Garrett]…is really a very exceptional child and it is a joy to teach her. In [N. Garrett] God has given you a precious gift. I have known her now over years, and she has never been different, as one finds at times with some children. I have also made enquiries at the school, and have been told that her marks have been up to 80%, which is far above the average child attending there, and the teachers said the same thing about her, how pleased they were with her work and what a fine child she was. I am writing this also to let you know that your own efforts in her earlier years have not been in vain, as a child of her age largely reflects the parents influence. Here your prayers for your child, and admonitions have borne rich fruit.

You remember while still in Alice Springs, how on various occasions I spoke to you about [N. Garrett] letting her continue at school and attend a College etc. I have also spoken to [N. Garrett] about it, and she is quite happy about the idea of becoming a school teacher, although she remarked but my Dad may not have enough money to pay for my education. However after making enquiries, I can now say that [N. Garrett]'s education will not cost you anything: the money needed is there for her. All I need to do is get your consent, then collect an estimate of the cost of her education, give school reports etc., and the matter is more less fixed up. So if the idea appeals to you would you please write and tell me so, and I shall go ahead.[39]

After this exchange, Albrecht prepared a statement, a draft of which appears in his papers:

To whom it may concern. My daughter, [N. Garrett], 14 years of age, has…now for over 4 years has attended the Public School in Alice Springs… I understand that she is well advanced, and she herself is keen to continue her studies, with a view of gaining the Leaving Certificate, and then go to the Teachers Training College. Unfortunately, being a labourer, I am unable to assist my daughter financially. However, I herewith declare my complete agreement with the aim my daughter has in view, and I would be grateful for any assistance that is given her. As far as I am concerned, I shall not in any way interfere with the education and training of my child, *with the one condition that she remains at liberty to discontinue and return home if and when for any reasons of her own, she wishes to do so.*[40]

N. Garrett travelled to live with the Kennedy family in Light's Pass, 1954. By 1960 she was attending a Nurses Aid College in Toorak, Melbourne.

78   Katherine Ellinghaus

The parents of N. Garrett were the first of many involved in the decision for their children to go South for education. In February 1958, Albrecht noted in a letter to the Headmaster of the Alice Springs Higher Primary School 'how more and more of the coloured people begin to appreciate a good education for their children, and show so much confidence in the school where they attend.' The letter was in relation to a boy who was boarding in Mparntwe while his parents 'live and work at Horseshoe Bend,' a cattle station 171 kilometres from the town.[41] In May the parents of two more girls applied to move their daughters from the school at the Bungalow to the Higher Primary School. Both girls were discussed by Albrecht, McCoy and by the Assistant Supervisor of Education in Darwin. One, who was seven years old, had been sent to the Bungalow because she was perceived as being of full descent, unlike her half-sisters who attended the Higher Primary School. The other girl, who was 12 or 13, was also the 'moving force' as Pearce described it, of her own education and wished to move from the school at the Bungalow to the Higher Primary School. Pearce reported that the girl had approached Albrecht several times before sending her father to speak with him. Albrecht was unable to convince her father, who offered money for food and books, that it was better for her to stay at the Bungalow School. Pearce was hesitant and wished for approval from Darwin; and the records do not show whether the girl was ever enrolled in the school of her choice.[42]

It is likely that there were many more parents and children in contact with Albrecht and asking for a chance to be educated beyond the school at the Bungalow, who did not leave a trace in the archive. In January 1959, McCoy wrote to Albrecht about a father, who had promised McCoy to send part of his earnings for the welfare of his son, left behind in Mparntwe to pursue his education.[43] In 1959, Albrecht was already lobbying the Lutheran Board about the need for a hostel for families who were 'conscious of the fact that their children have to be educated, otherwise it can happen that the Welfare Department steps in and removes the children.'[44] The records are patchy. But between March and May 1958, Albrecht filed the claims for Boarding Allowances for 14 children to travel South, and was organising Railway Concessions forms for their visits home.[45]

The influx of parents wanting education for their children, and children advocating for their own education, can be understood better in the context of the concept of 'imperial literacy.' Historian Tracey Banivanua Mar defined the concept of imperial literacy as a way of describing the many examples of colonised peoples becoming enthusiastic adopters of aspects of imperial culture in which they see value. Literacy, Banivanua Mar argues, was a common tool used by Indigenous peoples across the settler world for both accommodation and for protest.[46] Anangu people did not just want education because it might prevent child removal, but

Mparntwe and the Mission Block 79

also because it allowed them and their children not just to navigate the world in which they lived, but also to push back against it.

In the next chapter, we see how Albrecht's philosophies and actions pushed against the mainstream policies of the Australian government and, indeed, many other missionaries. As Tracey Banivanua Mar argued, many Indigenous people used missionaries and their teaching for 'varying purposes ranging from spiritual to functional; as tools of literacy or vehicles for travel; and as allies and diplomats for political and economic empowerment'. Banivanua Mar notes, though, that these tools were often ill-fitting and carried with them an 'intolerance that ensured colonialism was thoroughly and culturally insinuated into the lives of indigenous peoples'.[47]

Albrecht was undoubtedly part of a missionary worldview that supported colonialism, but his educational philosophy was more about preparing children for dealing with colonialism than it was about insinuating it into their lives. His scheme, though it took advantage of the policies and bursaries of the Northern Territory government, was driven by parents who also thought their children needed some measure of imperial literacy. In a world where the colonisers were not going away, and in which the rough cruelties of the Territory made it a challenging place for Anangu children to grow up, Albrecht saw himself as a bridge and a facilitator, one that stood between mainstream Australia and Anangu people. This chapter began by thinking about how Albrecht embodied the Enlightenment as he walked the segregated streets of Mparntwe in the postwar period, but it has also shown how Enlightenment ideas of progress and education played out at the local level, how the Enlightenment's emphasis on reason and individualism was taken up by Anangu parents in collaboration with a Lutheran pastor born in Germany but deeply embedded in multicultural town of Mparntwe (Alice Springs). We leave the story in late 1958, at the point where the first small group of girls were living with Lutheran families in rural areas where they attended local schools. These girls would soon come to the attention of some of the highest government administrators in Australia.

Notes

1 Paul Carter, *The Road to Botany Bay: An Essay in Spatial History* (London: Faber & Faber, 1987).

2 Katherine Ellinghaus and Leonie Stevens, 'Mind the Gap: Micro-Mobility, Counter Networks and Everyday Resistance in the Northern Territory in 1951,' *Journal of Colonialism and Colonial History* 19, No. 2 (Summer 2018), https://doi.org/10.1353/cch.2018.0013.

3 Everard Leske, ed., M. Lohe, F. W. Albrecht and L. H. Leske (contributing authors), *Hermannsburg: A Vision and a Mission*, revised ed. (Adelaide: Lutheran Publishing House, 2016), 106.

80 Katherine Ellinghaus

4 S. Parry and J. Wells, 'Schooling for Assimilation: Aboriginal Children in the Northern Territory, 1939–1955,' *History of Education Review* 26, No. 2 (1997): 49–63.

5 'Children Kept Away: Alice Springs Protest,' *Sydney Morning Herald*, 27 February 1951, 7; and 'Discriminatory Laws: N.T. Native Resentment,' *News* (Adelaide), 1 March 1951, 4.

6 Bruce W. Strong, 'Early Education in Alice Springs & "The Bungalow": 1800s to 1930s,' (Alice Springs: Bruce Strong, 2003), available at https://territorystories.nt.gov.au/10070/634097/0/9, accessed 26 June 2022.

7 F. W. Albrecht, 'Finke River Mission Newsletter,' Vol. 2, No. 1 (March 1955), Box 22, Finke River Mission archives, United Evangelical Lutheran Church in Australia (hereafter UELCA), Bowden, South Australia.

8 Anna Haebich, 'Imagining Assimilation,' *Australian Historical Studies* 118 (2002): 61–70.

9 The most important of these was the Welfare Ordinance (1953) which gave the Director of Welfare extensive powers over the lives of people declared to be 'wards.' Although the Ordinance made no reference to Aboriginality, the exception of people eligible to vote from the class of people that could be declared to be wards meant that it could only apply to Aboriginal people. See Russell McGregor, 'Wards, Words and Citizens: A. P. Elkin and Paul Hasluck on Assimilation,' *Oceania* 69 (1999): 243–259.

10 F.W. Albrecht to Director of Native Affairs, 17 March 1954, FRM Box 77, FWA-Corr (Non Board) Sept-Oct 1954, UECLA.

11 'Old Lutheran Church Alice Springs, 70th Anniversary, 1938–2008,' pamphlet, Lutheran Church of Australia (2008): 11–12.

12 Leske, ed., *Hermannsburg*, 107.

13 Leske, ed., *Hermannsburg*, 108.

14 Leske, ed., *Hermannsburg*, 108.

15 Leske, ed., *Hermannsburg*, 106.

16 Barbara Henson, *A Straight-Out Man: F. W. Albrecht and Central Australian Aborigines* (Parkville: Melbourne University Press, 1992), 221.

17 'Christmas & Newsletter 1958,' Box 22, UELCA.

18 Leske, ed., *Hermannsburg*, 106. See also F.R.M. Field Conference, 10 & 11 May, 1960, Alice Springs – South – Report, FRM Box 82, May–Dec 1960, UELCA.

19 Circular letter from L. Dodd, Assistant Supervisor of Education, Northern Territory Schools (WA- Corr (Non-Board) Jan–Mar 1956, BOX 78, UELCA.

20 Circular letter from L. Dodd.

21 F.W. Albrecht to Brother Zinnbauer, Lutheran City Mission, Adelaide, 21 September 1954, FRM Box 77, FWA-Corr (Non Board) Sept-Oct 1954, UECLA.

22 G. Briscoe, *Racial Folly: A Twentieth Century Aboriginal Family* (Canberra: ANU Press, 2010); C. Perkins, *A Bastard Like Me* (Sydney: Ure Smith, 1975); A. Mallett, *The Boys from St Francis* (Adelaide: Wakefield Press, 2018).

23 F. W. Albrecht to Lou A. Borgett, Esq, Maylands, SA, 8 October 1956, FRM Box 79, FWA Corr (Non-Board) Sept-Oct 1956, UELCA.

24 F. W. Albrecht to Brother Reuther, 29 March 1957, FRM Box 25 Albrecht Correspondence with Board 1955–58, UELCA.

25 F.W. Albrecht, 'Lutheran Hostel at Alice Springs,' May 1959, FRM Box 25, FW Albrecht Papers 1935–66, UELCA.

26 F. W. Albrecht to Brother Reuther, 13 September 1960, FRM Box 25 Albrecht Correspondence with Board 1955–58, UELCA.

27 F. W. Albrecht to Brother Reuther, 14 December 1960, FRM Box 25 Albrecht Correspondence with Board 1955–58, UELCA.

Mparntwe and the Mission Block 81

28 Albrecht, 'Lutheran Hostel at Alice Springs.'

29 F.W. Albrecht to Brother Reuther, 3 October 1958, FRM Box 25 Albrecht Correspondence with Board 1955–58, UELCA.

30 R.B. Reuther to Albrecht, 10 October 1958, FRM Box 25 Albrecht Correspondence with Board 1955–58, UELCA; F. W. Albrecht to Brother Reuther, 28 November 1958, Box 25 Albrecht Correspondence with Board 1955–58, UELCA; R. B. Reuther to Brother Albrecht, 19 December 1958, Box 25 Albrecht Correspondence with Board 1955–58, UELCA.

31 F. W. Albrecht to Brother Reuther, 22 December 1958; F. W. Albrecht to Brother Reuther, 6 January 1959; F. W. Albrecht to Brother Reuther, 14 January 1959, Box 25 Albrecht Correspondence with Board 1955–58, UELCA.

32 Corey W. Dyck, ed., *Women and Philosophy in Eighteenth-Century Germany* (Oxford: Oxford University Press, 2021); Katherine B. Clinton, 'Femme et Philosophe: Enlightenment Origins of Feminism,' *Eighteenth-Century Studies* 8, No. 3 (1975): 283–299; Barbara Taylor, 'Feminism and the Enlightenment 1650–1850,' *History Workshop Journal* 47 (1999): 261–272.

33 Henson, *A Straight-Out Man*, 212.

34 Victoria Haskins, 'On the Doorstep: Aboriginal Domestic Service as "Contact Zone,"' *Australian Feminist Studies* 16, No. 34 (2001): 13–25 and 'Domesticating Colonizers: Domesticity, Indigenous Domestic Labor, and the Modern Settler Colonial Nation,' *American Historical Review* 124, No. 4 (2019): 1290–1301.

35 Albrecht, 'Finke River Mission Newsletter.'

36 F. W. Albrecht, Alice Springs – South - Report, for period of May 1st, 1958, to September 15th, 1958, FRM Box 81, FWA Corr (Mar-May) 1958, UELCA.

37 Albrecht, 'Lutheran Hostel at Alice Springs.'

38 Henson, *A Straight-Out Man*, 212–213.

39 F. W. Albrecht to Mr & Mrs R. R. Garrett, Granite Downs, via Oodnadatta, S.A., 23 April 1953, FRM Box 76, FWA-Corr (Non-board) April 1953, UELCA.

40 Statement, unsigned, Witness F.R. Albrecht Sig. R. R. Garrett,' FRM Box 76, FWA-Corr (Non-Board) July–August 1953, UELCA. [my emphasis].

41 F. W. Albrecht to Mr Pearce, Headmaster, Alice Springs H.P. School 15 February 1958, FRM Box 81, FWA Corr (Mar–May) 1958, UELCA.

42 A. A. Pearce, Headmaster, Higher Primary School, Alice Springs to Assistant Supervisor of Education, Northern Territory Schools, 6 May 1958, FRM Box 81, FWA Corr (Mar–May) 1958, UELCA.

43 W. McCoy to Albrecht, 19 January 1959, FRM Box 82, FWA Corr (Jan Feb) 1959, UELCA.

44 Albrecht, 'Lutheran Hostel at Alice Springs.'

45 F. W. Albrecht to the Head Master, Alice Springs Higher Primary School, FRM Box 81, FWA Corr (Mar-May) 1958, UELCA.

46 Tracey Banivanua Mar, 'Imperial Literacy and Indigenous Rights: Tracing Transoceanic Circuits of a Modern Discourse,' *Aboriginal History* 37 (2013): 1–28. See also Tracey Banivanua Mar, 'Shadowing Imperial Networks: Indigenous Mobility and Australia's Pacific Past,' *Australian Historical Studies* 46, No. 3 (2015): 340–355; Tracey Banivanua Mar, *Decolonisation and the Pacific: Indigenous Globalisation and the Ends of Empire* (Cambridge: Cambridge University Press, 2016); Tracey Banivanua Mar and Nadia Rhook, 'Counternetworks of Empires: Reading Unexpected People in Unexpected Places,' *Journal of Colonialism and Colonial History* 19, No. 2 (Summer 2018), https://doi.org/10.1353/cch.2018.0009.

47 Banivanua Mar, 'Imperial Literacy and Indigenous Rights,' 7–8.

82 *Katherine Ellinghaus*

Bibliography

Primary

'Children Kept Away: Alice Springs Protest,' *Sydney Morning Herald*, 27 February 1951, 7.

'Discriminatory Laws: N.T. Native Resentment,' *News* (Adelaide), 1 March 1951, 4.

Finke River Mission archives, F. W. Albrecht Correspondence Files, Boxes 22, 25, 76–79, 81–82, United Evangelical Lutheran Church in Australia (UELCA), Bowden, South Australia.

'Old Lutheran Church Alice Springs, 70th Anniversary, 1938–2008.' Pamphlet, Lutheran Church of Australia, (2008): 11–12.

Strong, Bruce W. 'Early Education in Alice Springs & "The Bungalow": 1800s to 1930s.' (Alice Springs: Bruce Strong, 2003), available at https://territorystories.nt.gov.au/10070/634097/0/9, accessed 26 June 2022.

Secondary

Banivanua Mar, Tracey. *Decolonisation and the Pacific: Indigenous Globalisation and the Ends of Empire*. Cambridge: Cambridge University Press, 2016.

Banivanua Mar, Tracey. 'Imperial Literacy and Indigenous Rights: Tracing Transoceanic Circuits of a Modern Discourse.' *Aboriginal History* 37 (2013): 1–28.

Banivanua Mar, Tracey. 'Shadowing Imperial Networks: Indigenous Mobility and Australia's Pacific Past.' *Australian Historical Studies* 46, Number 3 (2015): 340–355.

Banivanua Mar, Tracey and Nadia Rhook. 'Counternetworks of Empires: Reading Unexpected People in Unexpected Places.' *Journal of Colonialism and Colonial History* 19, Number 2 (Summer 2018), https://doi.org/10.1353/cch.2018.0009.

Briscoe, Gordon. *Racial Folly: A Twentieth Century Aboriginal Family*. Canberra: ANU Press, 2010.

Carter, Paul. T*he Road to Botany Bay: An Essay in Spatial History*. London: Faber & Faber, 1987.

Clinton, Katherine B. 'Femme et Philosophe: Enlightenment Origins of Feminism.' *Eighteenth-Century Studies* 8, Number 3 (1975): 283–299.

Dyck, Corey W., editor. *Women and Philosophy in Eighteenth-Century Germany*. Oxford: Oxford University Press, 2021.

Ellinghaus, Katherine and Leonie Stevens. 'Mind the Gap: Micro-mobility, Counter Networks and Everyday Resistance in the Northern Territory in 1951.' *Journal of Colonialism and Colonial History* 19, Number 2 (Summer 2018), https://doi.org/10.1353/cch.2018.0013.

Haebich, Anna. 'Imagining Assimilation.' *Australian Historical Studies* 118 (2002): 61–70.

Haskins, Victoria. 'Domesticating Colonizers: Domesticity, Indigenous Domestic Labor, and the Modern Settler Colonial Nation,' *American Historical Review* 124, Number 4 (2019): 1290–1301.

Haskins, Victoria. 'On the Doorstep: Aboriginal Domestic Service as "Contact Zone."' *Australian Feminist Studies* 16, Number 34 (2001): 13–25.

Henson, Barbara. *A Straight-Out Man: F.W. Albrecht and Central Australian Aborigines*. Parkville: Melbourne University Press, 1992.

Leske, Everard, editor, M. Lohe, F. W. Albrecht and L. H. Leske (contributing authors), *Hermannsburg: A Vision and a Mission*. Revised edition. Adelaide: Lutheran Publishing House, 2016.

Mallett, Ashley. *The Boys from St Francis*. Adelaide: Wakefield Press, 2018.

McGregor, Russell. 'Wards, Words and Citizens: A. P. Elkin and Paul Hasluck on Assimilation.' *Oceania* 69 (1999): 243–259.

Parry, Suzanne and Julie Wells. 'Schooling for Assimilation: Aboriginal Children in the Northern Territory, 1939–1955.' *History of Education Review* 26, Number 2 (1997): 49–63.

Perkins, Charles. *A Bastard Like Me*. Sydney: Ure Smith, 1975.

Taylor, Barbara. 'Feminism and the Enlightenment 1650–1850.' *History Workshop Journal* 47 (1999): 261–272.

4 Enlightened Girls

The Scheme in Action

Katherine Ellinghaus

In February 1959, Australia's public radio and television broadcaster, the Australian Broadcasting Commission, reported that a conference of the United Evangelical Lutheran Church in South Australia had discussed a scheme in which Aboriginal children from Hermannsburg were hosted in southern homes of Lutheran Church members. The news item reported that there were already six young people living in the south and receiving 'training.'[1] In Canberra, staff in the federal government's Department of Territories sat up and took notice. This single news item had highlighted to the federal government the extent to which the Central Australian Lutherans were out of step with the biological racism and doomed race theory that dominated Australian thought in the first part of the twentieth century.

This chapter takes the Enlightenment ideas described in Chapters 1 and 2 and examines how they, transported to the unique context of Central Australia by Lutheran missionaries, resulted in a unique set of ideas about Aboriginal education. It sets Albrecht's ideas about education, and their expression in his scheme, against the prevailing ideas of the government of the day. The Enlightenment ideas held by Lutheran missionaries, and their emphasis on the value of culture, learning and education, personal duty and responsibility, put them in conflict with the cruel child removal policies of the government of post-war Australia. As the experiences of some of the first girls who went South show, Albrecht and his other mission workers demonstrated care and affection for these children, understood their individual needs and wants, including facilitating the need for them to continue their relationships with their communities and families.

When Albrecht's scheme came to the attention of the government in Canberra, its foreignness raised concern among the highest echelons of those in charge of the Northern Territory and Aboriginal Affairs. C. R. Lambert, the Secretary of the Department of Territories in Canberra, wrote to the Administrator of the Northern Territory asking for further information. J. C. Archer, Administrator of the Northern Territory from 1956 to 1961, replied to the Lambert's letter using the word 'disturbing.'[2] He named four of the children who had gone South with

DOI: 10.4324/9781003281634-5

Enlightened Girls 85

F. W. Albrecht's help, and noted that Albrecht 'apparently has in mind that the children will stay away from Alice Springs for only a short period – two to three years, will return to Alice Springs each holiday.'

The administrators anxiously discussed the details of Albrecht's scheme in a series of letters that now sit in a file in the National Archives. The Department of Territories was a Commonwealth government department, staffed by officials who were responsible to the Minister for Territories, Paul Hasluck. It was responsible for all of Australia's territories, including Papua New Guinea, Nauru, Norfolk Island and the Northern Territory, where Hasluck imposed his assimilationist ideas onto the Aboriginal population. Hasluck's version of assimilation was based on ideas of liberal individualism, and set him apart from other prominent assimilationists of the day, such as Professor of Anthropology, A.P. Elkin, who espoused a version where Aboriginal people could retain their cultural distinctiveness.[3] In this climate, it was unsurprising that Albrecht's scheme was a source of administrative dismay.

Albrecht's Scheme and Government Policy

Albrecht's views on education, developed in relative isolation in Central Australia and steeped in his essential Germanness and background in Enlightenment values of the pursuit of knowledge and individual progress, set him into direct conflict with the Australian government. Across Australia there was at this time a mostly symbiotic relationship between government and missions when it came to Aboriginal and Torres Strait Islander children. Missions took in children that governments removed, and in return were granted land on which to operate and financial subsidies.[4] Albrecht's philosophy ran counter to the government's cruel emphasis on child removal and cultural eradication.

Albrecht's efforts to send children south for education was not the problem. In fact, the Australian government had its own, similar scheme. In the early 1950s, the government and Church bodies had combined to create a scheme that sent selected mixed-descent children away from the Territory to be educated. Hasluck imagined the scheme would focus on 'lighter-coloured children who have no strong family ties,' and the government advertised widely in Church magazines seeking families to adopt, foster or sponsor children. Historian Anna Haebich estimates that by 1959 there were approximately 250 Northern Territory children being fostered or living in institutions or boarding schools in South Australia, Victoria, New South Wales and Queensland.[5] A 1964 government report described the government scheme as one

> whereby part-Aboriginal children from the Northern Territory may be transferred to institutions, boarding schools and foster homes in

86 Katherine Ellinghaus

southern states of Australia if it is considered that their transfer will afford them a greater opportunity for social development. The children are selected on the basis of their likely assimilation and their ability to profit from education and training.[6]

Many children were sent South without their parent's permission or sometimes even their knowledge.[7] Haebich reports that the experiences of children in the government scheme, which she estimates at being around 250 in 1959, were varied:

> It is impossible to say how many remained in the south although it would appear.... that many returned to the Northern Territory and to their Aboriginal families. Little is known about the achievements of these children – how many finished high school, took on apprenticeships, found labouring, factory or domestic work or simply dropped out of the system. It appears that only a small number went on to tertiary studies, where some found the pressure too great, while a distinguished few managed to achieve academic and public success.[8]

The Commonwealth government provided a subsidy of up to £300 per annum to pay the families or institutions who took in students, in addition to child endowment payments and Albrecht, perhaps naively, thought his students could access these payments as well. The Department of Territories was not so sure: Albrecht's scheme differed from theirs in a few fundamental ways. Archer grumbled that Albrecht was not following procedure by arranging inspection of the homes and a consultation with the prospective foster parents by a social worker from the Commonwealth Department of Social Services, nor did he obtain the Administrator's approval before he moved the children. The government was also concerned that the Lutherans had exposed one of the tensions that the 1953 ordinance created – the way it could remove government control over children, which was one of the foundations of government control of Aboriginal people. Hasluck's emphasis on assimilation was expressed in the 1953 Aboriginal Welfare Ordinance which made no reference to Aboriginality, but declared people who could not vote to be wards (which meant that it could only apply to Aboriginal people). The Ordinance gave the government enormous powers over the lives of declared wards.

What made the government nervous about Albrecht's scheme was that the children he was helping to educate were not under any government's legal control because they were of mixed descent. Those with any percentage of European or other 'blood' could not be declared wards. Archer wrote,

> Because these four children...cannot be declared wards the Director of Welfare could not prevent their removal from the Territory. Nor

Enlightened Girls 87

would the Director of Child Welfare have any power over them - he cannot act until a child has been declared a ward of the State under the Child Welfare Ordinance. The only persons who could have objected to the removal would have been the parents or those persons in loco parentis.[9]

Their status was also complicated because they had crossed into states that defined their Aboriginality differently.[10] Another point of contention was the age of the children – a common practice across the Stolen Generations was to remove pre-school aged children, even babies, from their families.[11] By contrast, in their early teens, Archer thought that '[t] hese girls seem too old to benefit educationally from their experience in the South.'[12]

Archer recommended a report on the 'condition' of the children and demanded that it be made 'abundantly clear' to the Finke River Mission authorities

> that there is a policy approval for training selected part-coloured people in the South and should the Mission wish to continue sending such children to the South they should work within the framework of the approved scheme and not embark on independent negotiations which could, in the long run, jeopardize Commonwealth/State relationships.[13]

Hasluck became more involved in July 1959, writing directly to Archer to 'ensure you are fully aware of the concern that is felt in Canberra' and threatening to report Albrecht to the South Australian authorities.[14] Albrecht, meanwhile, was reportedly concerned only with whether he could get financial support for the children under the government's scheme.

In August 1959, a welfare officer from Mparntwe was sent by the federal government to visit the five children who were living in South Australia. The Welfare Officer's report was positive, concluding that

> The training for homemaking which these girls receive will, we hope, create in them a desire for good home conditions…I feel that if only a small number of these girls can receive such training as Pastor Albrecht envisages they will on their return to the Northern Territory help the Welfare officers in their work of trying to raise the social standards of the part-coloured people.[15]

Welfare officers continued to check up on the children, and Albrecht encouraged the children to cooperate with them. In a 1961 letter to the girls, he informed them of an impending visit by a social worker from Adelaide:

> Miss Thompson has seen some of you already, and she will visit others as time goes on. She is a fine young lady, and if she comes to you,

88   *Katherine Ellinghaus*

I would ask you to show her that you have confidence in her and cooperate. She has been appointed for your good, and you can freely talk to her about anything that worries you: I am sure she will try to help you as much as she can.[16]

Hasluck himself summarised the fundamentally different views on assimilation that sat behind the official correspondence about the children's well-being and whether or not Albrecht could access financial assistance from the government. He thought that Albrecht might have had 'an imperfect understanding' of the purpose of the government's scheme, which was their 'ready assimilation':

If a child is more likely to find a happy and useful life as a normal member of the Australian community by being transferred from the Territory then we can assist the transfer. Although we should not be rigid in the way we plan the lives of other people, when we make the selection of a child as suitable for transfer there should be a reasonably high expectation that the child will never return to the Territory to live but will eventually "disappear" into the Australian community in the south. If it is just a matter of providing education for a future life in the Territory we can provide every opportunity inside the Territory itself. In this particular project we are concerned solely with the group who are likely to cross over from a coloured community into a general community.[17]

As we saw in Chapter 3, Albrecht's views about education were developed far away from Canberra and also in response to the particular coalition of Anangu parent's demands for education. No wonder they were an anathema to Hasluck and his ilk. Education had particularly been on Albrecht's mind since his first years in Mparntwe. In 1954, he penned a pamphlet entitled '75 Years of Schoolwork at Hermannsburg, Central Australia' which was published in the *Lutheran Herald* on Christmas day of that year.[18] In it, he charted the history of schooling at Hermannsburg which began in 1879 and finished with a long section entitled 'The Task Ahead' which argued, in blunt terms, that the way education for Anangu children was currently being approached in Central Australia was unhelpful. 'Generally speaking,' he wrote,

our school is still designed to give the child as good an education as is possible, but then expect[s] the child to take the step into life itself, choose a trade or some other calling in the same way as an ordinary white child. However we should know by now that this just will not work: past experience has taught us this abundantly.

Enlightened Girls 89

The reason why school was not a clear pathway into employment was not, as so many of Albrecht's generation thought, because Anangu people were incapable. Rather, Albrecht had a keen understanding of the reluctance, difficulties and cruelty of the 'imagined assimilation' that dominated Australian discourse at this point:

> It is obvious that the past of a people cannot be eradicated in a generation or two, neither is this altogether desirable. For instance, the nomadic instinct with many of them has remained quite a strong factor. Furthermore, our children still have their ideals largely in the bush; they think of the free life they enjoyed there, although it was not as free as it would appear on the surface. But with their feelings they continue to live in the past.[19]

Today, this passage might at first read as an expression of the mainstream, racist views of the day. The possessive 'our,' the reference to 'nomadic' lifestyles (so often used to denigrate), the concept of 'living in the past': these are phrases that nod to the ubiquitous racist assumptions of the period, which posited Aboriginal people as 'primitive' and 'backward.' Perhaps Albrecht was deliberately gesturing to those beliefs, which he must have known were held by so many of his readers. But buried between the lines is something else: an experience of, and perhaps even a respect and understanding of, the difference of Ananugu life – of its freedoms, of a past that was not 'primitive' but free of the cruelties and injustices of colonisation, and an understanding of the ridiculous fantasy that a few years of schooling would be enough to help Anangu children navigate the racist world of settler-colonial Australia, let alone the racist township of Mparntwe. Little had been done, Albrecht argued, to 'pave the way' for children to make the transition to a European way of life, to draw opportunities from the European culture that had invaded their lands, to make it 'inviting and attractive as possible.'[20]

There were practical as well as philosophical differences between Albrecht's ideas and the top-down government schemes operating in the Territory. Most significantly, the 'Part-Aboriginal Education and Training Scheme,' perhaps the closest policy to Albrecht's scheme, did not have a component which ensured that children could return to Central Australia after they had been sent south. Instead, the Minister was happy for the Director of Welfare 'to arrange for the employment of whichever of the methods – adoption, foster parents, school orphanage or other institution' on a case by case basis. This approach essentially gave government approval for people to move children South on an ad hoc basis. The only time the government seemed to worry about what these children would do after school was out of concern for prospective

90 *Katherine Ellinghaus*

foster parents who 'require to know whether it will be a long or short term placement.'[21]

Albrecht, by contrast, was not interested in the idea of permanent child removal. In 1956 he refuted rumours that he was involved in the 'picking up of [part-Aboriginal] children.'

> I have never missed an occasion to tell them how much better it is for such children, provided, of course, they are not neglected, if they are left at the stations where they were born and grow up. Afterwards, they not only fit into station life better, but, grown up away from the filth and temptations of town, are better men and women. By now they should begin to realise where an education leads to that is not above all regulated by the word of God.[22]

Albrecht's Christmas letter of 1959 outlined his 'new venture' of sending children south for two or three years, but emphasised that he did not

> favour a transfer for good; later on in life, in most cases such children feel they are out and away from their surroundings in which they grew up and where they will live later on. However, a term to give them the benefit of such a change can do them good that will last throughout their lives.[23]

Albrecht noted the importance of visits home at a Finke River Mission Field conference in 1960:

> Those 5 girls sent down early in 1959, all came back for the Christmas holidays. It was interesting to see with what warmth they were received by their relatives and how this brightened them up. It became so obvious that their feeling of belonging was now satisfied and they felt completely relaxed. For a sound and natural development of these children this is very necessary. One of them... who is about 17 now, has remained up here, but she has a very good position at station, where she does most of what has to be done in a house...from a report of others we understand that she herself had said she could never have attempted this work without the time she had had in the South.[24]

Albrecht disagreed with the assimilationist assumption that just placing children into mainstream schools would be enough to help them navigate the society that he no doubt found himself confronted with every day in Mparntwe: 'I am afraid the Gov. effort at present, though very well meant, is wasted simply by not taking into account sufficiently the peculiar position in which these children find themselves: they cannot be likened to a white child.'[25] In 1957, Albrecht wrote a response to a speech

Enlightened Girls **91**

made by a Mr Kearney in Wollongong (Albrecht gave no other details) in which he argued that the practice of placing Anangu children into white schools did not equip them with the skills they needed to flourish:

> Our schools, as they are constituted at present, do not prepare our Aborigine boys and girls for life. This is in no way a slur on the fine efforts made by most teachers, who give of their best. In my opinion, there is lack of understanding of the background of the Aborigines, and the system is wrong. [26]

The answer, Albrecht argued, was to keep children connected to their communities and their Country, although he expressed it in very different terms, describing an imagined Anangu lad:

> who has lived close to cattle camps all his life, knows how to ride any horse, enjoys outdoor life, is proud of his achievements. If such a boy still carried certain ideal of what his father has told him of times past, he has found something to replace and a level where he can hold his own against any white man, and be proud of it. [27]

Albrecht also noted that every child was different, and not all should be given the opportunity to assimilate:

> These people should be given training in every respect, and helped at all points to earn a living. At the same time, those very many who for some reason do not want to struggle under new conditions, these should be made to live in the bush - and there is plenty of it left in the Inland - and struggle there. [28]

Anangu people were not white, Albrecht argued, and

> [a]ny attempts to help them on lines we would assist white people must inevitably fail. But I have no doubt, if helped on lines that will take fully into account their peculiar make-up brought about by their life they have had to live by force of circumstances, they will become very valuable members of our Australian community, but only then. [29]

These ideas set Albrecht against the approaches favoured by the federal government and many other Churches and religious organisations. His ideas were also very different from those of most non-Indigenous Australians who, as Anna Haebich has described, either believed that children were better off living away from their families and communities or who were in a strange state of 'knowing and not knowing' about the systematic practice of child removal across the twentieth century. [30]

92 *Katherine Ellinghaus*

Enlightened Relationships

A key difference in Albrecht's approach was his individual knowledge of the people involved and the personal relationships he built and maintained with the children. Albrecht's 1960 Christmas letter showed how involved he was in the lives of the girls who had been sent South. He reported that all five girls had returned to Mparntwe for their summer holiday:

> All of them have improved in health: one of them had picked up as much as 28lbs in a little over 6 months. The three who continued at school all did well; one of them from the 26th position in class, came to be 11th, and one topped her grade. Parents and guardians were very happy about their children having been given this opportunity to live with people in the South, widen their experience and outlook. One of the girls, who is 17, has no intention of going back again, but all the others will, and are looking forward to it. [31]

Albrecht not only visited the girls while they were in the South, but sent circular letters to them giving news of home and of each other. He also used these letters to make holiday arrangements. Interstate travel was tricky and expensive at this time, and the Lutherans had to make complicated arrangements that involved train tickets, escorts and travel by truck to remote stations. His letters to the girls were personal, warm and encouraging of hard work. 'To those of you who have written to me, and many of you did, I send my sincere thanks,' he wrote to the girls participating in the scheme in September 1961,

> It has always been a real pleasure to receive your letters, and with many it was interesting to watch the steady progress you have made since you went away from here; your handwriting has improved.... your spelling, and your expression. It is well worth while, girls, to try and try hard. Even if it may seem to you that there is little progress you may rest assured that your effort never is in vain, there are always results, and so often very pleasing results. [32]

Albrecht used his circular letters to give news from home, showing how connected he was with the communities from which the girls came (Figure 4.1). A circular letter in 1961 by which time eight more children from the Finke River Mission had gone South, gave individual pieces of news about one girl's uncle, another's sister and congratulated another on being 'the most prolific letter writer.' It concluded:

> I hope you will all write again and let me know how you are. I often think of you all and pray for you that God may protect you from all harm and danger, bless you and make you a blessing for others. [33]

Figure 4.1 'The Mission Truck beside the Lutheran Church, Gap Road, Alice Springs, NT'. Courtesy of the Lutheran Archives.

In addition to using his letters for practical things, like facilitating contact between the girls, passing around addresses and organising for them to travel together, Albrecht also tried to guide their futures.[34] 'Among the people there is still a lot of drinking going on,' he reported of Mparntwe in 1961.

> I hope that you girls, when you come back later, and the time comes for you to get married, that you will make sure not to follow a drunkard. In the meantime pray to God that He will open the eyes of the men so they will see where this sort of life leads to and what terrible fruit such a life of sin yields.[35]

He constantly emphasised, sometimes bluntly, the importance of education, telling the story of one of the returned girls who did not get as far as he had hoped in school while in the South:

> if she had worked and got as far as the Progress Certificate, she would find it easier to find a job, and better pay. But as it is she has nothing to show, so is just left out. I trust that all of you will have this as your aim: the Progress Certificate. This is like a door opener for life, and we need many open doors to get on.[36]

In another letter, he wrote: 'one thing is certain: you will need every bit of education and training you can get. And this is the time of your life to get it.'[37]

Albrecht also used his letters to try to instil a sense of personal responsibility and gratitude in the girls:

> The most important thing, however, is that the Blessing of God is with us and in all we do. Dear children, do all you can to please those with

94 *Katherine Ellinghaus*

whom you stay; they are at this time like your parents, and it is through them that God blesses you. When you are home from school, try to help in the house without being asked first, and show your appreciation and gratitude for what they people do for you in every you can. ... One day you will reap the fruit of this; our God never forgets, and what we sow we also reap; from this fact nobody can get away.[38]

In another letter he asked them to have empathy for their host families. 'I would ask you girls to do what you can to show your gratitude to those who look after you,' he wrote to them all, 'You see, it is a very big thing if other people take strangers into their home.' Albrecht also emphasised how important it was for the girls to think about the continuation of the scheme, and their responsibility to ensure that their families might be willing to look after more children from Central Australia in the future. 'Each one of you can do so much', he urged, 'to make other people open their homes to more girls from up there, and one day you will even see more than now what this has meant in your life.' [39]

Albrecht, however, also acknowledged the difficulty of being away:

I know that some of you will have had days when you wished you were in the Centre, back where you were born and grew up. Such a transition from living conditions in the North to those in the South, is not without a few heartaches, and even disappointments. However, you will all admit that it all has been a wonderful experience to you, and that you have benefitted tremendously; the full extent of this will only come to you when you have gained a certain distance and see everything more distinctly.[40]

In his individual letters to the girls, Albrecht clearly expressed the Enlightenment ideals of personal autonomy and the potential of all human beings for self-improvement through education and hard work, imagining them playing out in the day to day attitude of his 'girls.' Lorna Wilson, Judd's mother, went South with her mother's blessing when she was 12 or 13 years old, and stayed for two years with a Lutheran family in Moculta. She then returned to Alice Springs for a year, then went South again, this time to St Paul's Lutheran College in Walla Walla, just outside Albury. Lorna became a nurse, then a language educator and cultural facilitator. She is deeply connected with her family, Community and culture. Albrecht wrote many letters to Lorna over the years she was in the South. In 1963, when she was enrolled at St Paul's Lutheran college in New South Wales he wrote:

Yes, try to work harder, there is no easy road to success but a good effort always finds its reward. I am glad to know you look up on your

Enlightened Girls 95

stay there as a God-given opportunity, which it is in every respect. Prey with us that God may open the way to many others to share with you in what is offered you there. God alone knows what your life will be when you are grown up.[41]

He often reminded Lorna of the way in which God was present in her life, and how the good works of those around her should be a model that she followed when she was an adult:

> I also loved to read about Mrs. Bethune who so willingly helped you with your clothing. Take this, too, Lorna as a gift from the hands of god and thank Him for it. We need such help on the way, we cannot do without it. But the amazing thing is, that, if we trust in God, He sees to it, and we are never found wanting. You are a stranger to this lady yet, she sees in you one whom God has sent to her. The day will come, Lorna, when you will be doing the same once you have completed your schooling and training. And then you will find out how such a service makes your life so much worth while, lifts you up into the presence of God. As you said in your letter, you thank God for everything every day in the morning and again at night. By doing this, you are keeping close to God.[42]

When Lorna graduated with her Intermediate certificate, Albrecht wrote to her again to give his congratulations, but also to emphasise that service to others and to god should be a part of her next steps. In essence, she should 'pay it forward':

> my hearty congratulations: you did it, and now the road is open for the next step, and then to wonderful service. Looking back on the part of your life's way, you will have deep gratitude to God for the way He has led you so far. And this will be ground for much more confidence for the future. Lorna dear, if you had not persevered in prayer and come to god with all your little and also not so little worries, you would never have made the grade. Ever so often in life we don't seem to feel the guidance and presence of God. Yet, He is near us all the time…With this I will say "kala" for the present. I read with interest of your further plans, which sound alright, especially since you have found such a good friend in Mrs. Bethune; we need such friends in life, and one day after you have established yourself, you will do the same and befriend others; it makes life so much more worthwhile.[43]

Although the scheme continued for decades, one early culmination of it was when Lorna Wilson and another girl from the scheme, now working

96 *Katherine Ellinghaus*

as nurses in Wodonga, NSW, paid their own way back to Mparntwe for a visit. Lorna Wilson remembered that

> When we told him that WE were going to pay your own way, he had tears in his eyes, because he knew, he knew, I think that we were had become independent and that we could understand that he put a lot of work into getting funding for us to be schooled and finding homes for us and a lot of things that like that so he was pretty pleased and had tears in his eyes.[44]

After so many years ensuring children were able to return to Central Australia, with all the cost and logistics, the significance of this moment is evidenced by its memorialisation in *The Lutheran* in 1968 (Figure 4.2).

Albrecht's scheme was, two years after he began it, approved by the Lutheran Synod in Adelaide, even after the difficulties with the Department of Native Affairs in Canberra. In response to that conflict, though, the Synod created a policy 'on sending natives South from the Finke River Mission.' The policy stated that while 'All are agreed that the experiment has been worthwhile and has proved to be beneficial' Albrecht was to keep both the Welfare Department and the Lutheran board fully

Figure 4.2 An excerpt from 'Success Story,' an article in *The Lutheran* in 1968 detailing the achievements of two of the scheme participants. Courtesy of the Lutheran Archives.

Enlightened Girls 97

informed at all times, and used language that was noticeably absent from any of Albrecht's writings. It included provisions such as:

> Any Native coming south will not leave the place to which he or she has been assigned by private arrangement. Where such a step is taken, and a Native has not honoured the purpose of his or her coming south, they shall be sent home forthwith. All must be done to impress upon these people that this is not a holiday or a walkabout. If a home proves unsuitable, then official arrangements shall be made to protect the interests of the Native.[45]

Albrecht's reply to this policy concluded that the scheme 'if fully developed...would be like the last stone in an arch, which completes the building.' He reminded the Synod that

> Our Church has done so much groundwork in the past, and I hope and pray that she will not be lacking in putting the last stone to it. We cannot get away from the fact that we serve the Kingdom of God by making them also useful members of the community in which we live.[46]

Albrecht's version of assimilation was thus different from some of his Lutheran colleagues, and the settler government. In a 1964 pamphlet, written a decade after '75 Years of Schoolwork at Hermannsburg', entitled 'Stages of Transition,' Albrecht pushed back again the idea of 'integration' and on behalf of the Lutheran Church raised 'a voice of warning against certain methods adopted at the present time' – this voice, he said, was drawn from 'our experience with Aborigines for more than 70 years.'[47] The current 'tendency at present to eliminate the vernacular, even frown on Aborigines speaking their own language' was wrong, Albrecht wrote. Young people, he thought,

> should be enabled to reach the stage where they can converse in English freely, they should also be encouraged and this for a considerable time to come, to retain their own language. If this is not done, the growing generation will become more and more unrooted. It becomes obvious already that the emphasis on English at all costs, has created, in many communities, a division between the older people and the growing generation, which is thus largely deprived of the steadying influence of the tribal leaders. There is much more in a language than expressing thoughts and conveying feelings.[48]

Albrecht's ideas about education were fully developed by 1964, and of course, by then, the scheme was already well underway and he had

98 *Katherine Ellinghaus*

organised more than twenty children to be sent South to live with Lutheran families and go to school. He was enthusiastic about apprenticeships/training schemes, but felt strongly that children should not just learn the curriculum but undertake training that would lead them to financial independence. He advocated that they stay at school until their 'training in European way of life' was sufficient – but this was not the assimilation policy of erasure practiced elsewhere: while he wanted white families to take children, it was only for a few years in their early teens and they must retain their language. He described the scheme in 1964 as the answer to the problem of finding a suitable education trajectory for Anangu children:

> A helpful step in this process of integration would be to encourage suitable white families to accept one or two Aborigine children into their homes, for a period of about 3 years, from the ages of 11 to 14 or 15. Such children would then be required to return to their parents, unless they have shown to have ability for further study.[49]

In 1965, Albrecht again publicly expressed his views that the current emphasis on assimilation, or, as he referred to it, integration, was missing the mark. As a member of a community who had been living and working with Aboriginal people for many decades, Albrecht felt driven (or as he put it 'under an obligation') to articulate the Church's 'attitude at this stage of transition.' He saw the present time as 'full of promise; yet, at the same time, so full of danger.'[50] In a pamphlet entitled 'Our Aborigines and the Australian Community' Albrecht insisted that Aboriginal culture was something to be proud of and retained:

> Since our Aborigines are a people with past which they have very reason to be proud of - their terrific struggle for an existence in an environment which was utterly hostile to them - cannot [but] evoke the admiration of everyone who knows it - they cannot be expected to forget this easily, nor expected to relinquish their way of life without experiencing great mental stress. Yet, that is what is asked of them....A number of white people in the South who have honestly tried to make the life of some Aborigine children happier by adopting them into their homes and families in the South, have been shocked because of their failure to achieve their objectives with them; such a sudden break was too painful for them to endure. We believe, therefore, that if this stage of the transition is hastened unduly, more harm will result.... We would strongly recommend that the Aborigines be allowed to continue their way of life, even if somewhat modified, and provided it is not contrary to the law of the country neither an offence against public health.[51]

Enlightened Girls 99

Albrecht stressed that the current manner of educating Aboriginal children was inadequate, and that a special curriculum and education system be created for them:

> We appreciate the splendid efforts made by our Commonwealth Department of Education, in trying to provide within the next few years adequate facilities to enable every [Aboriginal] child in the Territory to enjoy the benefits of a general education. We feel it our duty, however, to point out that a formal education as provided for white children is not adequate to equip the Native child for life.[52]

Albrecht drew on his experience of working closely with Anangu families, and in watching the difficulties faced by those children once they left whatever schooling they managed to obtain, completely unprepared for life as an Aboriginal person in the Northern Territory, which offered few opportunities for employment beyond labouring or domestic service in addition to racist views which saw Aboriginal people treated with shocking cruelty on an everyday basis. In this, Albrecht can be seen as a true 'Enlightener' – not one of the privileged philosophers of the movement, but one of the 'men of the world' written about by Roy Porter, activists who sought not just to understand the world though reason but to change it.[53]

The Finke River Mission's practice of facilitating children and teenagers to leave Mparntwe for education continued well into the 1980s. Once F. W. Albrecht retired it was continued by his son Paul Albrecht.[54] The first group of children to go South went on to work in a variety of places. N. Garrett became a nurse,[55] as did Lorna Wilson, and two other girls.[56] One girl worked in a Chemist shop in Mparntwe.[57] One boy, who attended St Paul's Lutheran College, was employed straight out of school 'in a clerical capacity with good chances of promotion at the Macquarie Ward Woollen Mills in Albury commencing 1969.'[58]

The children who participated in Albrecht's scheme were often lonely, homesick, and no doubt encountered racism and perhaps even cruelty in the South. Their scholarly achievements were not a magical ticket to a life free from difficulty or challenge. Nonetheless, their time in the South gave them experiences and qualifications that assisted them in navigating the racist world of post war Australia. The opportunities that Lutheran missionaries facilitated for Anangu children to gain an education without being separated, 'protected' from or simply removed from their families and communities was in sharp contrast to the extensive child removal taking place under the justification of 'education' all over Australia during the twentieth century.[59] No wonder it caused concern in the highest reaches of the Australian government, evidenced in the 1959 letter quoted at the beginning of this chapter in which Paul Hasluck, one of

100 *Katherine Ellinghaus*

Australia's most famous assimilationists, articulated 'the concern that is felt in Canberra' about Albrecht's scheme.

Perhaps this is why Albrecht himself was and is well loved by many of the children who participated in the scheme. As we have researched Albrecht's work, the authors have talked to many of the people who participated in the scheme as children. This book is part of a larger project that aims to write the history of Albrecht's scheme in ways that are meaningful to the participants themselves. In our discussions with participants in the scheme they have taken much care to emphasise that Albrecht, and later his son Paul, did not want to take their culture, language, or families away. They do not mince their words about the difficulties of being educated as children away from family, Country and community, but they have great respect and affection for many of those that facilitated those experiences, especially F. W. Albrecht. As Lorna Wilson remembered in an interview about her life in 2018: 'I think most of us, or all of us, loved that old man to bits because he treated us with a lot of respect and he got a lot of respect back.'[60]

Notes

1 Cecil R. Lambert to Administrator, Northern Territory, 23 February 1959, A452, 1959-739, Training of Aboriginal children from Hermansburg [Hermannsburg] Mission in South Australia, National Archives of Australia (hereafter NAA), Canberra.

2 James C. Archer to Secretary, Department of Territories, 3 April 1959, A452, 1959-739, Training of Aboriginal children from Hermansburg [Hermannsburg] Mission in South Australia, NAA.

3 Russell McGregor, 'Wards, Words and Citizens: A. P. Elkin and Paul Hasluck on Assimilation,' *Oceania* 69, No. 4 (1999): 243–259.

4 Anna Haebich, *Broken Circles: Fragmenting Indigenous Families 1800–2000* (Fremantle: Fremantle Arts Centre Press, 2000), 348–349.

5 Haebich, *Broken Circles*, 477–478.

6 'Northern Territory – Maintenance of Part-Aboriginal Children in Foster Homes and Institutions in Southern States of Australia,' A452, 1959-739, 31 January 1964, Training of Aboriginal children from Hermansburg [Hermannsburg] Mission in South Australia, NAA. Once the child turned eighteen, the funds dried up, unless the Minister himself approved an extension.

7 Haebich, *Broken Circles*, 479.

8 Haebich, *Broken Circles*, 481.

9 Archer to Secretary, Department of Territories, 3 April 1959. 'While powers of legal guardianship over all children were removed under the 1953 Ordinance, Aboriginal children under fourteen could still be removed by administrative decision and "mixed race" children with parental permission.' Haebich, *Broken Circles*, 462.

10 Archer to Secretary, Department of Territories, 3 April 1959.

11 'Children could be taken at any age. Many were taken within days of their birth (especially for adoption) and many others in early infancy. In other cases, the limited resources available dictated that the authorities wait until children were closer to school age and less demanding of staff time and skill.' Chapter 11 in

Enlightened Girls 101

National Inquiry into the Separation of Aboriginal and Torres Strait Islander Children from Their Families (Australia). Bringing Them Home: Report of the National Inquiry into the Separation of Aboriginal and Torres Strait Islander Children from Their Families (Sydney: Human Rights and Equal Opportunity Commission, 1997). https://humanrights.gov.au/our-work/bringing-them-home-report-1997, accessed 30 December 2022.

12 Archer to Secretary, Department of Territories, 3 April 1959.

13 Archer to Secretary, Department of Territories, 3 April 1959.

14 Paul Hasluck, Minister, to J.C. Archer, Administrator, 6 July 1959, A452, 1959-739, Training of Aboriginal children from Hermansburg [Hermannsburg] Mission in South Australia, NAA.

15 Mrs Archer, 'Report on Visit to Children placed in Foster Homes in SA by the Lutheran church,' 25 August 1959, A452, 1959-739, Training of Aboriginal children from Hermansburg [Hermannsburg] Mission in South Australia, NAA

16 F. W. Albrecht to 'Dear Girls,' 20 April 1961, FM Box 22, FWA Correspondence with Aboriginals, UELCA.

17 Minister to the Secretary, 'Transfer of Part-Coloured Children from the Northern Territory to South Australia by the Finke River Mission', 20 October 1959, A452, 1959-739, Training of Aboriginal children from Hermansburg [Hermannsburg] Mission in South Australia, NAA.

18 Box 25, Albrecht Papers, *Lutheran Herald*, UELCA.

19 F. W. Albrecht, '75 Years of Schoolwork at Hermannsburg, Central Australia,' November 1954, 8, FRM Box 25, FW Albrecht papers 1941–1964, UELCA. This was published in the *Lutheran Herald*: 'MISSION NEWS,' 25 December 1954, Box 25, Albrecht papers, Lutheran Herald, UELCA.

20 Albrecht, '75 Years of Schoolwork at Hermannsburg.'

21 Miss P. J. Thompson, Welfare Officer, Northern Territory Administration to Department of Interior, 13 December 1963, D4 082/4, Item NO. II-3/PA 'Part-Aboriginal Education Training Scheme,' NAA.

22 F. W. Albrecht to Mrs Stanes, 13 April 1956, FRM Box 78, FWA Corr (Non-Board) April-June 1956, UELCA.

23 F. W. Albrecht, Christmas Letter, January 1959, F1, 1958/1857 'Pastor Albrecht's Monthly Letters,' NAA.

24 F.R.M. Field Conference, 10 & 11 May, 1960, Alice Springs - South - Report, FRM Box 82, May-Dec 1960, UELCA.

25 F. W. Albrecht to Lou A. Borgett, Esq., 8 October 1956, FRM Box 79, FWA Corr (Non-Board), Sept-Oct 1956, UELCA.

26 'Some Comments on reported speech by Mr. Kearney at Wollongong,' 12/2/57, FRM Box 25, Albrecht Correspondence with Board 1955–1958, UELCA.

27 'Some Comments on reported speech by Mr. Kearney at Wollongong.'.

28 'Some Comments on reported speech by Mr. Kearney at Wollongong.'

29 'Some Comments on reported speech by Mr. Kearney at Wollongong.'.

30 Anna Haebich, 'Between Knowing and Not Knowing: Public Knowledge of the Stolen Generations,' *Aboriginal History* 25 (2001): 70–90.

31 F.W. Albrecht, 'The Finke River Mission in 1959', FRM Box 22, FWA Christmas Letters, UELCA.

32 F. W. Albrecht to 'Dear Girls,' 1 September 1961, 'FWA Correspondence with Aboriginals,' UELCA.

33 Albrecht to 'Dear Girls,' 1 September 1961.

34 Albrecht to 'Dear Girls,' 20 April 1961.

35 Albrecht to 'Dear Girls,' 20 April 1961.

102 *Katherine Ellinghaus*

36 Albrecht to 'Dear Girls,' 20 April 1961.
37 F. W. Albrecht to 'Dear Girls,' 24 April 1962, FWA Correspondence 1961–1965, UELCA.
38 Albrecht to 'Dear Girls,' 20 April 1961.
39 Albrecht to 'Dear Girls', 24 April 1962.
40 F. W. Albrecht to 'Dear Children,' 6 December 1961, Box 22, FWA Correspondence with Aboriginals, UELCA.
41 F. W. Albrecht to Lorna Wilson, 9 October 1963, FWA Correspondence, 1961–1965, UELCA.
42 F. W. Albrecht to Lorna Wilson, 14 March 1965, Box 22, FWA Correspondence, 1961–1965, UELCA.
43 F. W. Albrecht to Lorna Wilson, 29 November 1965, Box 22, FWA Correspondence, 1961–1965, UELCA.
44 Interview with Lorna Pamela Wilson, 13 February 2018.
45 'Policy on Sending Natives South from the F.R.M,' FRM Box 25 Albrecht Correspondence with Board 1959–1961, UELCA.
46 F. W. Albrecht, 'Some Comments on the Policy on Sending Natives South from the FRM,' FRM Box 25 Albrecht Correspondence with Board 1959–1961, UELCA.
47 F. W. Albrecht, 'Stages of Transition,' January 1964, Box 25, F.W. Albrecht Papers, 1935–1966, UELCA.
48 Albrecht, 'Stages of Transition.'
49 Albrecht, 'Stages of Transition.'
50 Rev. F. W. Albrecht, M.B.E., 'Our Aborigines and the Australian Community,' 1. Box 25, F. W. Albrecht Papers, 1935–1966, UELCA.
51 Albrecht, 'Our Aborigines and the Australian Community,' 1.
52 Albrecht, 'Our Aborigines and the Australian Community,' 3.
53 Roy Porter and Mikulas Teich, eds., *The Enlightenment in National Context* (Cambridge, NY: Cambridge University Press, 1981).
54 Interview with Rhonda Inkamala and Lorna Wilson, 31 May 2018.
55 F. W. Albrecht to Brother Reuther, 3 October 1958, FRM Box 25 Albrecht Correspondence with Board 1955–1958, UECLA.
56 M. C. Taylor to ? 4 October 1966, D4082-WB377, NAA.
57 F. W. Albrecht to Lorna Wilson, 9 October 1963, FWA Correspondence, 1961–1965, UECLA.
58 H. C. Giese, Note for file, 9 May 1968, 'Robert Taylor', D4082-WB377, NAA.
59 *Bringing Them Home.*
60 Interview with Lorna Pamela Wilson, 13 February 2018.

Bibliography

Primary

A452, 1959-739, Training of Aboriginal children from Hermansburg [Hermannsburg] Mission in South Australia, National Archives of Australia, Canberra.

Finke River Mission archives, F.W. Albrecht Correspondence Files, Boxes 22, 25, 76–79, 81–82, United Evangelical Lutheran Church in Australia (UELCA), Bowden, South Australia.

Interview with Lorna Pamela Wilson, 13 February 2018.

Interview with Rhonda Inkamala and Lorna Wilson, 31 May 2018.

'Robert Taylor', D4 082-WB377, National Archives of Australia, Canberra.

Enlightened Girls 103

Secondary

Haebich, Anna. 'Between Knowing and Not Knowing: Public Knowledge of the Stolen Generations.' *Aboriginal History* 25 (2001): 70–90.

Haebich, Anna. *Broken Circles: Fragmenting Indigenous Families 1800–2000.* Fremantle: Fremantle Arts Centre Press, 2000.

McGregor, Russell. 'Wards, Words and Citizens: A. P. Elkin and Paul Hasluck on Assimilation.' *Oceania* 69, Number 4 (1999): 243–259.

National Inquiry into the Separation of Aboriginal and Torres Strait Islander Children from Their Families (Australia). Bringing them Home: Report of the National Inquiry into the Separation of Aboriginal and Torres Strait Islander Children from Their Families. Sydney: Human Rights and Equal Opportunity Commission, 1997. https://humanrights.gov.au/our-work/bringing-them-home-report-1997, accessed 30 December 2022.

Porter, Ray and Mikulas Teich, editors. *The Enlightenment in National Context.* Cambridge, New York: Cambridge University Press, 1981.

Conclusion

Katherine Ellinghaus and Barry Judd

The history of Aboriginal children living away from their families and communities is often one of sadness, loss and cruelty, dominated by the story of the Stolen Generations. This is because the history of 'modern' settler-colonial Australia is dominated by the widespread removal of Indigenous children from their families. As historian Peter Read argues:

> it used to be said that by the end of the first world war, there wasn't a single British family that had not been touched, by injury or death, by the fighting in Europe. It is probably fair to say that except for the remotest regions of the nation, there was not a single Aboriginal family which had not been touched by the policy of removal. Everybody had lost someone.[1]

The story of the missions to the Aborigines commenced by the Old Lutherans of South Australia and of the educational scheme in Central Australia that Albrecht devised and operationalised raises many questions about how we might write histories of children moving away from family, the history of Aboriginal education, how we assess the cultural and political nuances of assimilation or acculturation. And indeed, how we come to assess and write the history of the settler-state of Australia overall. The histories that we outline in this book push up against many of the larger stories professional historians and Indigenous Studies scholars who work in Australian academia construct about assimilation policies and their application in the work, training and education of Indigenous peoples. It does not fit into broader narratives about missions and the role Christian Churches played in the propagation of the Stolen generations. Or about our ideas about the power and agency that Aboriginal people, including children, exercised in their lives to make choices and exercise a degree of freedom albeit within the constraints of coercive policies and practices. Our purpose in writing this book is not to discount or diminish these histories, but to add nuance to them. We have sought to bring the politics

DOI: 10.4324/9781003281634-6

Conclusion 105

of voice and location to centre stage, and by doing so, give a different perspective not just on Australian history but also on how we might see the European Enlightenment and the ideas it generated as something whose reach extended far beyond Europe and into the individual lives of Aboriginal people living in twentieth-century Central Australia.

Our first chapter addressed the complex ways in which we understand the traces the Antipodean expression of Lutheranism embodied by missionaries who travelled from Germany to Central Australia in the seventh decade of the nineteenth century. We examined how their work with *Arandaic* and Western desert linguistics, cultural beliefs and practices in Central Australia engaged with both Lutheran theological and Enlightenment ideas and values that emphasised vernacular culture and language, learning and education, personal duty, and responsibility (work ethic). We did so to draw attention to the fact that the Lutheran missionaries in Central Australia, in their work with and understanding of the Aranda, Luritja and Pitjantjatjara, were not directed by the notions of biological hierarchy and Social Darwinism that justified the killing of Indigenous peoples in the interest of settler-colonialism in Australia. In this chapter, we demonstrated that Lutherans, including men like Kempe, Strehlow and Albrecht, viewed their working relationships with Aboriginal people through a cultural framing of the world that understood human differences according to relative cultures that had been shaped by divergent historical trajectories. We argued that these perspectives have a genealogy that may be traced back to the German Enlightenment and the ideas popularised by Herder and Hegel. We did so to emphasise that the Old Lutherans and the German missionaries who led the Finke River Mission were interested in vernacular cultures in ways settler-colonial Anglo-Australia was not. Overwhelmingly, settler-colonial Anglo-Australia was only interested in the idea of race (and the practice of racism) as a mechanism and framework to denigrate Aboriginal peoples. Race and racism used in this way has been the intellectual handmaid to the logic of Anglo-Australian settler-colonialism and its logic of eliminating Aboriginal peoples from the continent now known as Australia.

Chapter 2 focused on F. W. Albrecht's life and the development of his personal mission to the Aranda, Luritja and other Anangu peoples with whom he worked. We explored how Albrecht's childhood and early adulthood immersed in the world of the German Empire and of a German culture that had been shaped by the twin ideas of Lutheranism as well as the Age of Enlightenment and how these specific cultural influences that were Central to his personal identity in turn shaped his interactions and secular agenda of work with Aboriginal peoples in Central Australia. Albrecht was both challenged by and, in turn, challenged the religious and government institutions with which he engaged in his time

106 *Katherine Ellinghaus and Barry Judd*

at Hermannsburg mission. During the interwar years of the twentieth century, he became preoccupied with what he called the "problem of work" as his schemes to assimilate Aranda men into the national and global capitalist economies were constantly frustrated by traditional economic traditions that emphasised resource sharing and immediate consumption. Significantly, although Albrecht was never able to reconcile these differences in economic values, he never gave up in his efforts to overcome the "problem of work" as he regarded economic integration through training and employment as critical to securing Aboriginal futures. In this Albrecht and his Lutheran mission once again stand in stark contrast to settler-colonial Anglo-Australian government who, since assuming sole control of setting the terms of relationships between settlers and Aboriginal peoples in Central Australia in the 1970s, has given up on the concept of viable Aboriginal integration into the regional, national and global economics of capitalism. Whereas Albrecht never deviated from the idea that paid work would provide a pathway to secure Aboriginal futures, Australian governments at national and territory levels have seemingly condemned Aboriginal people to a present charactered by endless welfare dependency, poverty, ill health and social disfunction.

Chapter 3 addressed the period of Albrecht's life after he moved to Mparntwe (Alice Springs) from Ntaria (Hermannsburg) to care for his ailing wife. At the Finke River Mission in Mpartnwe, Albrecht continued his mission work and expressed his ideas about individualism and religion through co-designing, with local parents, a scheme designed to offer choices and education to individual children. Chapter 4 described the scheme itself, the government's reaction to it, and tells the story of some of the children who participated in its first years. The scheme placed Albrecht in conflict with the Australian government and its ideas about who Aboriginal people should be and how they should behave. This chapter examined how Albrecht's Enlightenment beliefs and values pushed back against common understandings of the project of assimilation in post- World War II Australia. These two chapters, taken together, tell the story of a locally run, ad hoc education scheme that impacted on a relatively small number of Aboriginal people. By tracing the origins of that small scheme back through its Lutheran founder and to the Enlightenment philosophies he was trained in and which shaped the way he and his fellow missionaries interacted with the Anangu people they met and lived with in Central Australia, we hope we have shown the different possibilities that existed even at the height of the assimilationist period in Australia. In directly contrasting it with government schemes of education from the same period, aimed at the same cohort of children, we also aimed to show how differently education could look for Aboriginal children in a scheme that was shaped in negotiation with parents and families and was informed by a rudimentary – but still greater than most mainstream

Conclusion 107

Australians Aranda – understanding of the way those communities worked and what skills and experiences might best assist Aboriginal people in negotiating Anglo-Australia.

What lessons might we learn from this story? And what does it mean for the place that Aboriginal people, culture, knowledges and ideas might occupy in contemporary Australia, a society that owes so much to the central tenets of European Enlightenment? By putting the story of the Lutheran missionaries who worked in Central Australia into an Enlightenment frame, we have aimed to construct an understanding of the Central Australian past that shifts Australian history writing beyond telling stories of racism and treating Aboriginal peoples as if they exist as nothing more than one-dimensional cartoon characters, as stereotypes of race. Our objective has been to give our historical subjects agency, freedom, autonomy, duty and responsibility, and acknowledge the complexity and value of their cultural and linguistic traditions. Aboriginal people in Central Australia, like people everywhere in the world, are extremely complex and therefore unpredictable in ways that simplistic formulations of race and racism do not accept or consider as real.

Albrecht held a qualified view of assimilation which deemed that it was only good and only right when it occurred with the consent of Aboriginal people themselves. This meant his view of consent was underpinned by both his understanding of Lutheran theology and his immersion into a German national culture where Kantian ideals of freedom and autonomy, duty and responsibility were well known and influential. He developed personal, caring relationships with the children that he worked with, and those feelings were often reciprocated. The Old Lutheran Church in Mpartnwe is now a living museum, a place where photographs of Albrecht, his family, the Mission Block, the pastoral stations he visited and the people who came into his orbit are displayed on the walls and copied into folders that can be flicked through by visitors.[2] Unlike most Indigenous exhibitions in museums and libraries around Australia, these visitors are mostly not well meaning non-Indigenous people coming to learn about settler-colonialism, but the Aboriginal people connected to that history themselves, come to reminisce about their childhood experiences in the Lutheran Church and to reconnect with their own and their family's histories. Here, in the stone Church built on Arrernte randa land in Mpartnwe, is a part of the history of the European Enlightenment or more specifically the German Enlightenment that rarely gets included in the mainstream Eurocentric historical narrative.

We hope this book prompts readers to think about the Australian past in ways that are not shaped by the framework of biological race and the racist mistruths that emerge from such ways of thinking when considering relationships between Aboriginal peoples and those who came to the southern continent from the late eighteenth century to the present time.

Figure 5.1 Lorna Wilson and Katherine Ellinghaus in the Old Lutheran Church, Mparntwe (Alice Springs), May 2021. Photograph reproduced courtesy of Katherine Ellinghaus.

While the European Enlightenment and the liberal political traditions and free market economic systems it has spawned have become easy targets for those who oppose settler-colonialism in Australia and elsewhere, the ideas of Enlightenment have also provided Aboriginal peoples with opportunities to liberate themselves from the coercive power of states and the oppressive workings of historic global processes such as settler-colonialism. The story of F. W. Albrecht and of the Old Lutherans of South Australia and the commitment to engage with Aboriginal people in Central Australia through mission is something all Australians should know about. While settler-colonial Anglo-Australia speaks the language of reconciliation, Albrecht and the Old Lutherans lived it. In the 'new' Church in Alice Springs today services are delivered in Aranda, Luritja and Pitjantjatjara in a building where Aboriginal cultural values are embedded into the structure through artworks that showcase the unique and now globally famous art forms of Central Australia. Aboriginal pastors

Conclusion 109

work alongside non-Indigenous clergy throughout the region as the work of the Finke River Mission continues a relationship that commenced in 1877. The work of Albrecht and his adherence to Lutheran theology and ideas from the German Enlightenment that had become embedded in German cultural perspectives and shaped his world view provided the Aboriginal peoples with whom he worked with the opportunity to become fully functional human beings in a settler-colonial context shaped by race and racism that positioned them as inferior caricatures and representative of a savage race whose time in Australia had now passed. For this reason alone his work and his insights into training and employment and education in respect of Aboriginal people need to be not only remembered but celebrated (Figure 5.1).

Notes

1 Peter Read, 'The Return of the Stolen Generation,' *Journal of Australian Studies* 22, No. 59 (1998): 9.
2 Helen Beringen, 'The Treasure Hunter,' Lutheran Church of Australia, 1 February 2019, https://www.lca.org.au/the-treasure-hunter/, accessed 5 March 2023.

Bibliography

Beringen, Helen. 'The Treasure Hunter.' Lutheran Church of Australia, 1 February 2019, https://www.lca.org.au/the-treasure-hunter/, accessed 5 March 2023.
Read, Peter. 'The Return of the Stolen Generation.' *Journal of Australian Studies* 22, No. 59 (1998): 8–19.

Index

Note: *Italic* page numbers refer to figures and page numbers followed by "n" denote endnotes.

Aboriginal children 2, 16, 19, 62, 69, 72, 84–86, 99, 104, 106
absolute idealism (Hegelism) 36
Adelaide 21–22, 48, 58, 72, 87, 96
agency 8, 19, 23, 61–62, 104, 107
Albrecht, Friedrich Wilhelm 5–8, 10, 17–19, 26–29, 38, 48–50, 67–71, 84–85, 104–109; aboriginal futures 51–55; Christmas letter 71, 77, 90, 92; economic freedom and cultural autonomy 55–62; education scheme 68–69, 72–79, 85–90; problem of work 57, 106; relationships with scheme participants 92–100; scheme and government policy 85–91
Anangu 5, 22, 67–73, 75–76, 78–79, 88–89, 91, 98–99, 105–106
Angas, George Fife 21
Aranda 22–27, 48–50, 52–62, 70–71, 105–106, 108
Archer, J. C. 84–87
assimilation 3–6, 26, 54, 58, 60–62, 69, 74, 85–86, 88–90, 97–98, 104, 106–107
Austin-Broos, Diane 57–58

Banivanua Mar, Tracey 78–79
biological determinism 3–5
Blainey, Geoffrey 16–17, 39n4

Canberra 69, 84, 87–88, 96, 100
Christianity 16–17, 21–26, 50–51, 61, 67, 73, 75, 104

colonialism 1–3, 17–27, 51–52, 57–58, 60–62, 79, 104–108
Commonwealth government 85–86
consent 5, 8, 54, 60–62, 77, 107

Darwin, Charles: *On the Origin of Species* 3–4
Department of Territories 84–86
dying race theory 51–52

education 30, 68–69, 72–79, 85–90
Ellinghaus, Katherine 9–10, *108*
Enlightenment 1–6, 8, 10, 17–20, 22, 27–38, 49, 51, 53, 60–62, 75–76, 79, 84–85, 94, 105–108

Finke River Mission 16–17, 22–27, 38, 48–50, 52–55, 58, 61, 68–71, *70*, 73, 90, 92, 96, 99, 105–106, 109
Flanagan, Richard 7, 12n23
Frederick William III of Prussia 20–21

Geist 36
German Enlightenment 4, 8, 18, 27–38, 49, 51, 53, 60, 105, 107, 109
Groundwork of the Metaphysics of Morals (Kant) 33

Haebich, Anna 69, 85–86, 91
Hasluck, Paul 57, 85–88, 99–100
Hegel, George Wilhelm Frederick 32–33, 35–38, 51–53, 105;

112   *Index*

The Phenomenology of Spirit
36–37
Henson, Barbara 57–58, 71, 75–76
Herder, Johann Gottfried von 32–38,
50–53, 105
Hermannsburg 5–6, *9,* 16–17, 19,
22–27, 38, 48–59, 62, 67, 69,
75, 97, 106
Hitler, Adolf 8, 32
Humboldt, Alexander von 34

imperial literacy 78–79
Ingkarta 48, 67

Judd, Barry 7–8, 10, 16

Kant, Immanuel 20, 32–38, 49,
53, 107; *Groundwork of the
Metaphysics of Morals* 33
kinship 4, 10

Lambert, C. R. 84
Langton, Marcia 23
Lockwood, Christine 40n19
Luritja 8, 19, 23–27, 35, 38, 48, 50,
52, 55, 105, 108
Lutheran Church 16, 21, 23, 29, 31,
37, 49, 54, 84, *93,* 97, 107
Lutheranism 4–10, 16–38, 48–56, 61,
68, 71–73, 75–76, 78–79, 84,
88, 105–109
Luther, Martin 25, 27–34, 37–38, 52

Macquarie, Lachlan 2–3
Mahood, Kim 23
McCoy, W. 78
McGregor, Russell 5
mission: Finke River 16–17, 22–27,
38, 48–50, 52–55, 58, 61,
68–71, *70,* 73, 90, 92, 96,

99, 105–106, 109; Lutheran
4–5, 16–27, 48–49, 84, 99,
105–107
Mparntwe 67–79, 87–90, 92–93, 96,
99, 106

Namatjira, Albert 19, 56–58, 60

Old Lutheran 20–27, 37, 48, 59, 61,
104–105, 107–108, *108*
On the Origin of Species (Darwin)
3–4

The Phenomenology of Spirit (Hegel)
36–37
Pitjantjatjara 19, 23–24, 48, 50, 52,
57, 61, 67, 105, 108
Porter, Roy 99
Prussian Union 20–21

racism 1–5, 7, 10, 17–19, 51–52, 61,
70, 84, 99, 105, 107, 109
Read, Peter 104
Reuther, R. B. 73–74
Rousseau, Jean Jacques 2, 34

Scheibel, Johann Gottfried 21
Schürmann, Clamor Wilhelm 22
Spencer, Walter Baldwin 26
Strehlow, Carl 25–26
Sturm und Drang movement 34

Table of Duties 30–31
Teichelmann, Christian Gottlieb 22
Tjukurrpa 24

Welfare Ordinance (1953) 57, 80n9,
86–87
Whitlam, E. G. 4
Wilson, Lorna 94–96, 99–100, *108*